How Millionaires

STAY *Rich* FOREVER

Retirement planning secrets of millionaires and how they can work for you!

Secrets on how self-made millionaires secure their wealth!

J. M. TRIPPON, CPA
The Millionaires' Retirement Planning Advisor

BRETTON WOODS PRESS LLC

BELLAIRE, TX
www.stayrichforever.com

HOW MILLIONAIRES STAY RICH FOREVER
Retirement Planning Secrets of Millionaires
and How They Can Work For You!
by J.M. Trippon CPA

Cover and text design © TLC Graphics, www.TLCGraphics.com

Bretton Woods Press, LLC
5959 West Loop South #510
Bellaire, TX 77401

ISBN: 0-9723389-1-8
Library of Congress Control Number: 2003110478

TABLE *of* CONTENTS

INTRODUCTION

BUILDING WEALTH

MAINTAINING WEALTH

TAX EFFICIENCY

DISABILITY AND ESTATE PLANNING

FINAL THOUGHTS

INTRODUCTION

If I could teach you the secrets to how self-made million-aires create their wealth, and the techniques they use to keep it secure during retirement so that they never have to worry about running out of funds during their lifetime, would you be willing to spend a few hours learning how?

One of the most important truths I have learned over the past twenty years as a CPA and financial advisor is that success leaves a "trail of clues" which can be followed. I say this with confidence because over the past 20 years I have personally met with, consulted or advised over a thousand millionaires. This book is about what I have learned from their personal stories, many of which are told inside these pages. The prob-lem for the average person is that often by the age they learn to identify the "trail of clues," they have already passed the opportunity to turn this knowledge into great wealth.

After reading this book you will have a pretty clear idea how self-made millionaires first acquire, and then mange to hold onto their wealth, in spite of high tax rates, fluctuations in the stock markets, and the litigious world we live in. As one of my millionaire clients says, her primary finan-cial goal is to always maintain enough wealth to "live a life of simple elegance." This book will show you how it is done.

Are you the skeptical type? That's OK with me. Keep reading anyway, and by the end of this book I think I will have made a believer out of you. The only thing I ask is that you pay close attention and keep an open mind.

MY STORY

I have been a CPA and financial advisor for over twenty years. About fif-teen years ago I decided to leave the comfort and predictability of working for Price Waterhouse, the international CPA and consulting powerhouse, to start my own firm. I wanted to work with individuals, business owners and corporate executives to help them achieve their financial goals while achieving my own goal of running a practice the way I thought it should be done.

I have never had trouble attracting clients because I am incredibly passionate about creating increased value in my client's lives through what I do for them. So soon after opening my firm, I found myself very busy helping clients improve their financial affairs and better structure their tax planning.

At that time I did not offer investment selection and management services but instead I would create my clients' financial, tax and budget plans and then refer them to one of several local stockbrokers for implementation.

I quickly became disillusioned with what I saw. Many of the stockbrokers were ignorant on even the basics of comprehensive financial planning.

They seemed to have no interest in doing anything other than making the largest commissions in the shortest period of time.

They did not want to spend the time to make sure the investments they were selling would be either the most cost effective or even efficient for their clients' tax position. They did not understand the proper use of advanced risk management techniques to safeguard the assets against market declines.

I realized pretty quickly that I needed another solution for my clients. Ultimately, my concern for my clients, together with my frustration with the available options for the ethical implementation of my planning, led me to become licensed to select and manage investments.

Today, in addition to owning my CPA firm, I also manage a branch of Raymond James Financial Services, Incorporated, a member firm of the National Association of Securities Dealers (NASD) and the Securities Investor Protection Corporation (SIPC.) This business structure allows me to both devise plans for my clients and implement the plans in a proper, ethical, and cost sensible way.

My typical client is over age 50 and has investment assets of between $1 million and $10 million. When I share with you a specific strategy or technique for the creating and maintaining your million dollar portfolio, I am not telling you some theory about what I think might work. I am sharing with you what I know works based on actual experience. Better yet, I am showing you exactly how to apply it to your personal situation.

Regardless of whether you and I ever meet, I believe you will benefit from the lessons I will share with you as I have gone through the evolution of my professional career. What you will learn should make you savvier about your money, and when you interview potential financial advisors, it should make it easier to find one who is a good fit for you.

WHO SHOULD READ THIS BOOK?

This book is written for people in their 50s, 60s and 70s who desire financial security and want to maintain a high quality of life in retirement. This book is also written for those younger people who are curious about how millionaires set the stage for lifetime wealth and then maintain it.

Are you already a millionaire? If you are, congratulations! This book is for you and will help you keep it that way. The biggest challenge many people face after acquiring a million dollar net worth is preserving it from a myriad of risks including stock market declines, divorces, lawsuits, taxation, healthcare costs, and investment scams. We will cover each of these areas in detail and I will show you the best ideas I have seen for building and preserving wealth for retirement.

Are you not yet a millionaire but want to be? This book is also for you. In these pages you will learn the techniques and secrets I have observed in over one thousand millionaires I have met over the past 20 years. I will reveal the best habits I have seen for building wealth. I will also discuss the quickest ways to lose your money once it has been accumulated, so that you can avoid making mistakes that have cost others their fortunes.

TEN REASONS YOU NEED THIS BOOK

1. You could go several lifetimes and never meet a thousand millionaires who were willing sit down with you and not only share their stories about how to build and hold onto wealth, but also show you how to apply their lessons to your personal circumstances.

2. Financial security is critical to your personal dignity and future independence.

3. People are living longer. According to a recent study, the fastest growing age group in the USA is the age group 100 and over.

4. No other book of this type exists. It is based on real case studies and client interviews conducted over a 20-year period.

5. What you don't know can hurt you.

6. Social security is an inadequate source of retirement income.

7. It helps the reader be sure there are no gaps in their own retirement planning.

8. It is wiser to learn from others' failures than to make the mistakes in your own life.

9. You will be a wiser financial steward of the financial opportunities you are presented with.

10. You don't have to be a millionaire to learn from them because success leaves a "trail of clues." The book will show you how to detect them, and then apply then in your own life.

THE PURPOSE

My purpose for this book is to teach you the secrets of how self-made millionaires create their wealth. Additionally, I want to teach you the techniques millionaires use to keep their finances so secure during retirement that they never have to worry about running out of money during their lifetime.

I strongly believe that financial security is critical to personal dignity and independence. I cannot guarantee that this book will make you a millionaire or prevent you from ever suffering a financial loss. We do not control everything in our lives but we do have the ability to control much more than most of us make the decision to control.

If you are open minded, and are up to my challenge, I can guarantee you will learn the best secrets and techniques I have seen used to accumulate and maintain wealth. These are the same secrets and techniques that have worked for thousands of millionaires. They will work for you, too.

So let's get started.

J.M. Trippon CPA
Soli Deo Gloria

CHAPTER I

The Stay Rich Philosophy

Make the most of yourself, for that is all there is for you.
– RALPH WALDO EMERSON –
POET

There is a dangerous school of thought being advanced by many of today's financial pundits and retirement-planning advisors. It is a philosophy that can destroy your wealth and force you back to work during your retirement years. It is the philosophy of "asset-spend down."

The "asset spend down" theory was dramatically illustrated by the popular, but in my opinion, misguided 1990s book, "Die Broke." Essentially, my understanding of the author's point was that

- you can't control the future (true),
- you can't depend on the stock market (certainly true over the short run),
- retirement is a relatively recent invention (arguable depending on your position on the economic food chain) and, therefore
- you should plan on working until you are no longer able and then die broke (remember "your last check should be to the undertaker...and it should bounce"?)

The book justifies its intellectual drivel by reminding us, "you can't take it with you anyway."

Although most financial planning firms would not easily concede that they follow the "asset spend down" philosophy, let' s take a closer look at how they advise you to plan for your retirement.

If you go to most any financial planner or financial planning website, you will find a formula to calculate how much money you will need to live comfortably in retirement.

Inherent in that calculation are assumptions about your life expectancy (although you are rarely told what they are assuming your lifespan to be.) The assumption they make is that you do not need to Stay Rich Forever and then project a spending down of your assets over an estimated period (your remaining years).

Well, I beg to differ with the "asset spend down" approach. I believe the only sensible approach to planning for retirement is radically different. The only sensible approach in planning for your retirement is to utilize a philosophy that ensures your financial well being will continue uninterrupted

(1) No matter what the stock market does and

(2) No matter how long you live.

This is how millionaires stay wealthy after they retire.

> **The Stay Rich Forever mindset is to believe that we will always need money and; therefore, we cannot ever spend down our principal.**

If the stock market declines of the past five years have taught us anything, it is that we need more money to retire on than we ever thought we would. We have also been painfully reminded that stocks do not go up in a straight line and that, in any given year, we have no assurance of what our equity portfolios will be worth 12 months later.

So you better have a plan to deal with uncertainty! If you planned a spend-down of your assets during your life, any hiccup in the stock market or a protracted bear market could wipe out your reserves and leave you scratching your head and asking what happened to your nest egg. I want you to have a rewarding retirement, whether or not you live it as a millionaire. Our journey to retirement must therefore begin with a question:

WHAT DOES RETIREMENT MEAN TO YOU?

What is retirement? It certainly isn't what it used to be!! Rather than a brief period between working and death, retirement often spans a much longer period of time and reflects very active and diverse lifestyles.

> **It is important that you set financial goals for retirement because, more than in any other period of life, finances will dictate your lifestyle. Setting these goals is highly personal and no one else can do that for you. You must set your goals and determine your priorities, deciding for yourself what's important. The goal of this book, therefore, is not to determine how you retire, but to show you how to maintain or increase your current standard of living at retirement. Forever.**

As you can imagine, there are as many different financial goals as there are people. Regardless of where you want to be and how you want to live, you can learn from the best practices of the wealthy in preparing for retirement. Why reinvent the wheel? I see no need to beat your head against a financial brick wall trying to figure out what works, do you? The following charts show what millionaires had to say when we asked, "Do you work with a financial or tax advisor?"

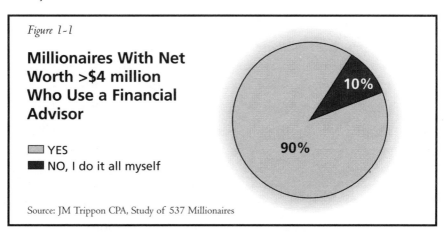

Figure 1-1

Millionaires With Net Worth >$4 million Who Use a Financial Advisor

- ▢ YES
- ■ NO, I do it all myself

10%

90%

Source: JM Trippon CPA, Study of 537 Millionaires

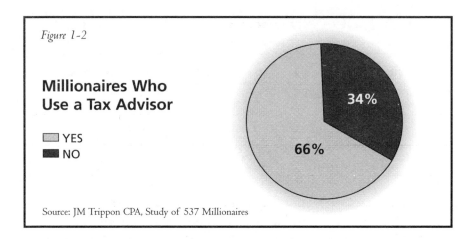

Figure 1-2

Millionaires Who Use a Tax Advisor

▨ YES
▨ NO

34%

66%

Source: JM Trippon CPA, Study of 537 Millionaires

After working with over a 1,000 millionaires, I know the secrets they use to maintain a wealthy retirement lifestyle. These are not "get rich quick" schemes, but tried and true, long term, reasonable risk strategies that will keep you living at the standard you desire. How? First, look at the issues that concern you and the goals you want to achieve such as:

- Financial independence
- Travel
- Retirement location
- Health concerns
- Reaching a lifelong dream
- Paying for grandchildren's education

This list is by no means exhaustive. Everyone is different so your goals for retirement should reflect your personal lifestyle. If you envision traveling around the world and maintaining a couple of houses, your investment income needs will greatly exceed those of your neighbor who plans to stick close to home and do volunteer work. In reality, there is no one "right" answer, because we all have different goals for retirement. So, let's start by listing your retirement goals.

List your retirement goals here:

_____

_____

_____

_____

_____

_____

_____

_____

_____

_____

_____

_____

_____

_____

_____

_____

_____

_____

_____

_____

_____

_____

After determining your retirement goals, you will need to create a plan to achieve them. Retirement is no longer what it once was. People are living longer, healthier, and more active lives well beyond what used to be retirement age. Your investments must reflect these changes and keep pace with your dreams. So let's give up on the old school approach of "Die Broke."

Let's structure our lives to Stay Rich Forever!

CHAPTER 2

Meet Our Millionaires
Your Introduction to the Four Pillars

Making money is a hobby that will complement
any other hobbies you have, beautifully.

– SCOTT ALEXANDER –
WRITER

Over the past 20 years I have been the financial and tax advisor to some of America's wealthiest families. In doing so, I personally met and interviewed over 1,000 millionaires. When you meet so many wealthy people, interesting trends emerge and one of the most interesting was that the rich generally share the same habits.

To test this observation, I began an in-depth process of surveying and questioning millionaires. The result is this book, which is based on my interviews with these retirement-age millionaires.

The millionaires I interviewed came from every walk of life. Some were college educated with advanced degrees, but it may surprise you to know that others did not even finish high school. Although many lived in Texas, I found that the same habits were shared by retirement-age millionaires in the states of California, Colorado, Florida, New York, and Washington.

Research conducted in 2003 indicates that out of over 100 million families in the U.S., at least 7 million[1] are millionaire families. In my hometown of Houston, Texas, we have approximately 127,000 millionaires. I am blessed to be in a rewarding profession that puts me in contact with these interesting people on a daily basis.

(1)   Source: Merrill Lynch/Cap Gemini Ernst & Young,
World Wealth Report 2003 p.23

They say that your first million is the toughest to make. I certainly agree because I have witnessed this in what so many of my clients gone through to create their fortunes. But I have also witnessed how difficult it is to protect and to preserve wealth, especially in uncertain times. To "Stay Rich Forever," we must not only know the techniques for acquiring wealth, but, perhaps more importantly, we need to know how to maintain it.

So what can we learn from the millionaires I interviewed and the habits they share? The answer is that we can learn their methods and mindset and apply them to ourselves.

THE FOUR PILLARS

If our goal is to erect a house (or should I say mansion) that generates a lifetime of wealth, we need to build in upon a solid foundation. In a perfect world, the wealth we create can span multiple generations, and so the house we build must be supported by four pillars, which are the ability to:

- **Create and Grow Wealth**
- **Protect and Preserve Wealth**
- **Receive Income in Tax Efficient Ways**
- **Protect Wealth in Times of Disability and After Death**

If you refer back to the table of contents, you will note that this book is organized into four sections, one for each of the four pillars. This structure will help us to focus on the requirements of each of these areas.

You will also become familiar with charts like the following:

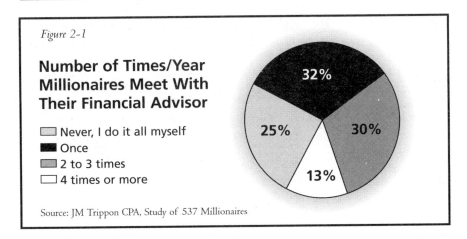

Figure 2-1

Number of Times/Year Millionaires Meet With Their Financial Advisor

- Never, I do it all myself
- Once
- 2 to 3 times
- 4 times or more

32%
30%
13%
25%

Source: JM Trippon CPA, Study of 537 Millionaires

These charts will tell you more about the millionaires we interviewed and will reveal the thinking of our millionaires to illustrate how they Stay Rich Forever!

MILLIONAIRE STORIES

Although I know you will learn a lot from the charts in this book, this book is not intended to simply be a compilation of statistics. To derive the greatest benefit from our time together in this book, you must do more than just read it. You must internalize its message, accept it, and then live it.

To help, I have included over 25 "millionaire" and "former millionaire" stories.

In each example, I will introduce you to millionaires (and former millionaires) who I have worked with, describe their situations, and then draw lessons from the decisions they have made.

Through this process, you will you learn how making smart monetary decisions can accelerate the accumulation of your wealth and, perhaps even more importantly, you will learn how making poor decisions about money can destroy your financial security.

DO MILLIONAIRES WORRY ABOUT MONEY?

You bet they do! According to our interviews the biggest concerns of retirement age millionaires in order of importance are:

CONCERNS OF RETIRMENT-AGE MILLIONAIRES
1. Running out of money
2. How to manage their investments
3. Taxes

In interviews with non-millionaire retirees, the answers were virtually the same. So let's get started! Our first step, taking inventory, consists of identifying where you stand financially today.

CHAPTER 3

Taking Inventory
Our First Step

*To do anything truly worth doing, I must not stand back shivering
and thinking of the cold and danger, but jump in with gusto
and scramble through as well as I can.*

– OG MANDINO –
MOTIVATIONAL WRITER & SPEAKER

Preparing for retirement is similar to getting ready for a trip. In order to know what to pack, you must know where you are going! Where are you starting? What is your destination and what do you want to do once you get there? When do you plan to leave?

Where you begin and where you go will determine whether you travel by train, boat, or jet. What you want to do when you arrive will help you determine what to pack. If you were going to a formal affair, you would feel awkward wearing jeans and a T-shirt!! And when you want to leave will determine how soon you should purchase tickets, reserve rooms, and make all the other arrangements necessary for a great trip.

These same considerations apply to retirement planning.

1. Where are you starting?
2. Where do you want to end up & what do you want to do when you get there?
3. When are you going to begin?

The first question asks where you presently stand. It covers your savings, work related pension plans, investments, and all other income as well as all debts and monthly spending requirements. So, begin by listing your annual income, which can be in the form of paychecks, trust funds, dividends, etc. Then figure out your expenses. Some people find it useful to put their expenses into categories, but like goals, these categories differ for everyone!!

It may surprise you to learn that the millionaires we have interviewed have become so familiar with their spending habits, they no longer maintain a written budget.

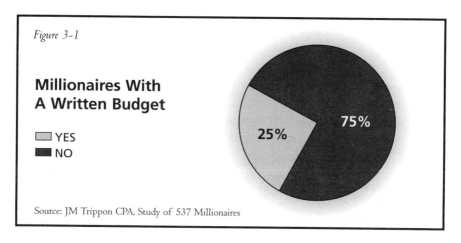

Figure 3-1

Millionaires With A Written Budget

☐ YES
■ NO

25%   75%

Source: JM Trippon CPA, Study of 537 Millionaires

Interestingly, our research indicates the more wealthy people become, the less attention they give to budget issues.

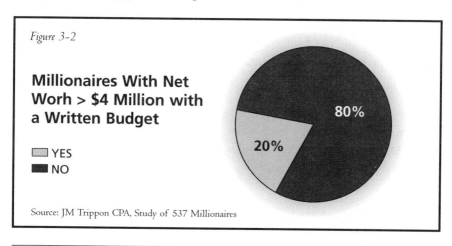

Figure 3-2

Millionaires With Net Worh > $4 Million with a Written Budget

☐ YES
■ NO

20%   80%

Source: JM Trippon CPA, Study of 537 Millionaires

Since you are spending a few hours with me, reading this book, we can presume that you care enough about your future to make sure your finances are in order. So you need to take inventory of where you are now. Fillout the financial inventory form below to get a clear idea where your finances stand today.

Figure 3-3	**FINANCIAL INVENTORY**

ASSETS
    Cash on Hand   _____
    Checking Account   _____
    Savings Account   _____
    CDs   _____
    Investment Accounts (non retirement)   _____
     Stocks   _____
     Bonds   _____
     Mutual Funds   _____
    Retirement Accounts   _____
     Stocks   _____
     Bonds   _____
     Mutual Funds   _____
    Cash Value of Life Insurance   _____
    Cash Value of Annuities   _____
    Market Value of Home   _____
    Market Value of Other Real Estate   _____
    Collectibles (market value)   _____
    Auto (market value)   _____
    Other assets   _____
           TOTAL ASSETS   _____

LIABILITIES
    Credit Cards   _____
    Consumer Lines of Credit   _____
    Auto Loans   _____
    Mortgage Debt   _____
    Margin Loans   _____
    Other Debt   _____
           TOTAL LIABILITIES   _____

NET WORTH (ASSESTS MINUS LIABILITIES)   _____

Now go back to the start of this chapter and look at our second inventory question. Where are you going in retirement, and what do you want to do when you get there? This is where your retirement goals come in. List your retirement income and your retirement expenses. Will the retirement budget cover your projected expenses? If not, where will you get the necessary money ?

Figure 3-4	**RETIREMENT INCOME & EXPENSES**	
		ANNUAL AMOUNT
INCOME		
Dividends		_____
Interest		_____
Pensions		_____
Rental Income		_____
Salaries		_____
Self-Employment		_____
Social Security		_____
Other (itemize)		_____
	TOTAL INCOME	_____
EXPENSES		
Income Taxes (Federal & State)		_____
Alimony/Child Support		_____
Auto Payment		_____
Auto (gas & maintenance)		_____
Auto Insurance		_____
Charitable Contributions/Tithe		_____
Clothing		_____
Credit Card Payments		_____
Education		_____
Entertainment, Hobbies, and Vacations		_____
Food		_____
Gifts		_____
Health Insurance		_____
Housing		
Mortgage or Rent		_____
Property Taxes		_____
Utilities		_____
Homeowners/Renters Insurance		_____

Figure 3-4 **RETIREMENT INCOME & EXPENSES (CONT.)**

	ANNUAL AMOUNT
Liability Insurance	_____
Long Term Care	_____
Maid	_____
Medical Deductibles	_____
Other Debt Payments	_____
Personal Care	_____
Miscellaneous	_____
TOTAL EXPENSES	_____
SURPLUS OR SHORTFALL (INCOME LESS EXPENSES)	_____

Finally, when do you plan to start your retirement? How many years do you have to close any gap between your current income and the income you will need for your retirement?

At this stage we are only gathering data. We will examine what to do with this information in our next chapter.

If you have a shortfall of income I know you may be worried about it. Be patient, we will roll up our sleeves and come up with some solutions to deal with your shortfall soon.

CHAPTER 4

When Should I Retire
How Much Money Is Enough
to Retire Comfortably

I've got all the money I'll ever need, if I die by four o'clock.
— HENNY YOUNGMAN –
COMEDIAN

The starting point for every millionaire's retirement planning is knowing how much wealth is needed to retire comfortably. This knowledge is both fundamental and critical.

SO HOW MUCH IS ENOUGH?

The simple answer is that it depends on your budget.

> **You will have enough money for retirement when, on an "inflation adjusted basis," you can maintain your chosen lifestyle without decreasing your investment principal.**

I once had a client, a 70-year-old medical doctor, who could not afford to retire in spite of having maintained a net income of over $200,000 for at least 25 years. After a lifetime working, he had not managed to accumulate enough to stop working and maintain his lifestyle. He never did retire. When he passed away (at age 70) from a heart attack, which was likely facilitated by financial stress, he had just come out of bankruptcy and was virtually penniless. His wife ended up moving in with one of their children.

On the other hand, I am seeing a growing number of people retire in their 40's and 50's with multimillion dollar portfolios. In fact, one of my clients, though not yet retired, has built a million dollar net worth in only ten years. The techniques he used have been included in this book.

> **Perhaps most revealing, I have numerous clients in their 50's and 60's who retire happily and comfortably without having a million dollar investment portfolio.**

The formula I use to determine if a client has adequate funds to retire is shown below.

You have enough money to retire when:

$$
\begin{array}{r}
\text{Pensions} \\
+ \text{ Social security} \\
+ \text{ Investment returns estimated at 4 to 6\%} \\
\text{per annum (net of inflation)} \\
\hline
> \text{ or } = \text{ Budgeted Needs}
\end{array}
$$

What? Investment returns calculated at 4 to 6%? Isn't that too conservative? Absolutely not! Remember that to maintain wealth we must first keep up with inflation. Long-term inflation historically runs 2 to 3.5% per year. So, when I say that I am estimating income at 4 to 6% per annum (net of inflation), what I am really saying is that my goal is to design a portfolio that has the potential of earning 6 to 9.5% per year on a gross pre-inflation basis.

I do not believe that anyone should plan for retirement using a spend down of principal approach that is based on a particular estimated life expectancy. In other words, don't bet that you are going live for a certain number of years and hope that you die before your money runs out. Unfortunately for many financial pundits this is a radical idea.

Remember again the recent bestseller entitled "Die Broke?" Die Broke? Well, dying broke works wonderfully only if you know the exact future date of your death. In my opinion, this type of "pop culture" trash-investment advice can get you into serious financial trouble.

With my philosophy, we assume that you will live forever and live only off your inflation-adjusted income. If you do, you will never run out of money, which is the name of the game.

Do you know the fastest growing age group in the United States? Care to guess? People over age 100 are the fastest growing age group in the United States. Yesterday I met with one of my clients who went to visit her grandmother. Grandma still lives by herself and maintains her own home at the age of 104. Age 104!

Retirement planning is intended to make sure that your money lasts. Not everyone lives to age 104, or wants to, but you may. So it's essential to make sure that your money keeps you company!

ACTION STEPS

1. Prepare a budget
2. Verify that your budget covers the required tax liability on whatever income you will need.
3. Using my income formula determine if you have sufficient income to retire.
4. If you have sufficient income to retire, congratulations, you are on the right track.
5. If you do not enough to retire, change your budget, keep working—full or part time, or adjust your portfolio balance within acceptable risk parameters.

The above action steps are healthy to go through at any time. As you get closer to retirement, however, we need to be on a more specific timetable to avoid making expensive mistakes.

TIMETABLE

If you are getting ready to retire, follow a timetable and begin preparations at least 2 years in advance.

24 Months Before Retirement

- Prepare a Budget
- Review debt plan
- Interview investment advisors

18 Months Before Retirement

- Hire an investment advisor for at least 25% of your portfolio
- Develop an investment policy statement

13 Months Before Retirement

- Accumulate a written copy of company benefits policies

12 Months Before Retirement

- Begin Tax planning with CPA

9 Months Before Retirement

- Reevaluate investment advisor against goals

8 Months Before Retirement

- Complete advisor team

6 Months Before Retirement

- Accumulate company retirement forms
- If considering additional life or health insurance — go through underwriting

3 Months Before Retirement

- Review rules for company stock options with CPA & investment advisor

8 Months Before Retirement

- Open rollover IRA
- Complete purchase of any new life/health or disability policies

45 Days Before Retirement

- Submit retirement forms to benefits department
- Set up direct deposit and tax withholding for retirement payments

BUILDING WEALTH

CHAPTER 5

Long-Term Savings Plan

Success is the sum of small efforts,
repeated day in and day out...
— ROBERT COLLIER —
WRITER

The most consistent difference between people who become millionaires before they retire and those who do not is that the millionaires have developed the long-term habit of saving. In more than twenty years of working with millionaires and their finances, I have noticed their tendency to save so many times that I have finally taken it for granted.

"Money" magazine published a study in its August 2000 edition which reported that approximately 100 million families in the U.S. Of this group, 7 million families are millionaires and 93 million are not. Although this may not be surprising, what is worthy of note is that 80% of the millionaire families were self-made.

The secret of wealth (that so many people miss) is that in America, almost anyone with a moderate level of discipline can become a millionaire. To become a millionaire, you do not have to be a surgeon or the chairman of the board of a major corporation. You do not even have to hold a high paying job. You must, however, be disciplined enough to save money year in and year out on a consistent basis.

Albert Einstein once called compound interest: "The greatest mathematical discovery of all time."

MILLIONAIRE STORY

Lesson: Long Term Savings Plans Work

NAME:	Don
AGE:	58
NET WORTH:	$2.4 million

Don, a retired client of mine, is in his late fifties and is a multi-millionaire. He never made more than $60,000 a year while working and never went to college. No, Don did not inherit his money or marry an heiress.

Don did not have be a surgeon to retire a millionaire; he simply needed to be consistent in saving at least $3.87 a day. Early in his working life Don developed the habit and today he is a millionaire. I have worked with many surgeons who are older than Don who still haven't saved their first million.

The following table shows the amount of investment and the time it takes to accumulate $1 million at a 10% compound interest rate.

Figure 5-1	**YEARS TO MILLION AT**		
AGE	AGE 65	MONTHLY INVESTMENT	DAILY INVESTMENT
20	45	116	3.87
25	40	179	5.97
30	35	292	9.73
35	30	481	16.03
40	25	805	26.83
45	20	1,382	46.07
50	15	2,491	83.03
55	10	5,229	174.30

This is a hypothetical illustration and is not intended to reflect the actual performance of any particular security.

What separates the spenders from the savers? In their 1996 book: *The Millionaire Next Door*, professors Thomas Stanley and William Danko studied prices paid by millionaires for typical purchases. Here are some facts they discovered:

Most ever spent by an average millionaire for a:

MEN'S SUIT:	$399
WRISTWATCH:	$235
PAIR OF SHOES:	$140
NEW AUTOMOBILE:	$29,000

If you study these facts, you will quickly surmise that most millionaires are relatively frugal people. By limiting their luxuries they are able to save consistently over long periods of time.

Let's take a closer look at the proper way to build long-term wealth. The millionaires I have met generally:

1. Are not flashy with their wealth.
2. Would rather shop at Wal-Mart than Neiman Marcus.
3. Live by the rules of hard work & disciplined saving.
4. Have stable family lives.
5. Live a debt free life.

Most millionaire are cautious spenders and do not live the extravagant lifestyle the media presumes. They would rather have their money generate a profit than spend it. Take a look at our chart on the following page which shows how often female millionaires go to the beauty salon.

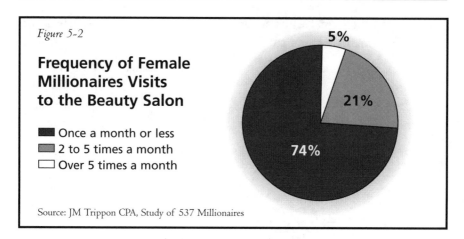

Figure 5-2

Frequency of Female Millionaires Visits to the Beauty Salon

- Once a month or less
- 2 to 5 times a month
- Over 5 times a month

5%

21%

74%

Source: JM Trippon CPA, Study of 537 Millionaires

Millionaires have learned how to live on their "Income" and not on their "If-Come." We will explore this millionaire habit in our next chapter.

CHAPTER 6

Frugality
Living on "Income" & Not on "If Come"

If your outgo exceeds your income,
then your upkeep will be your downfall.
– BILL EARLE –
WRITER

If saving is the most consistent difference between those who acquire and maintain significant wealth and those who do not, then living frugally is the catalyst that creates the ability to save. We need to live on our "Income" and not spend based on impulse or wishful thinking. If we spend based on "If-Come", we will never build and maintain lifetime wealth. In truth, we actually have to live on less than our income because, logically, if we spend everything we make, there can be no savings.

Living a frugal lifestyle is a long-term habit of many of the millionaires I have interviewed. In fact, they have been living frugally for so long that many no longer keep a written budget because their spending habits have become ingrained as a part of who they are.

Many people assume that millionaires have private chefs or never cook at home. But as you will see in the following chart, millionaires are just not big spenders.

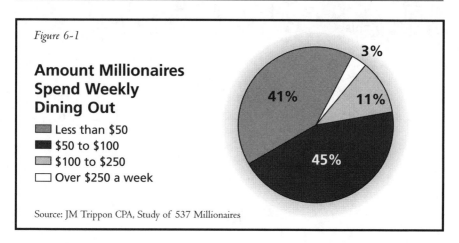

Figure 6-1

Amount Millionaires Spend Weekly Dining Out

- Less than $50
- $50 to $100
- $100 to $250
- Over $250 a week

3%
41%
11%
45%

Source: JM Trippon CPA, Study of 537 Millionaires

A penny saved is a penny earned. Although we have all heard that expression, it is not entirely correct. A penny saved is MORE than a penny earned. How in the world do I, a CPA, figure that?

Well, first take a look at your tax bracket, which with the ever-changing tax laws can be tricky. However, let's say for the sake of argument, that by the time you pay all your taxes—federal, social security, state, local— you are paying about 50% of your income to the government!! This is true for many of us. OUCH!

In practical terms, what does this mean to you? If you are paid $1000, you take home $500. Under this scenario, Ben Franklin would have said that a penny earned is only half a penny saved.

So, how does saving make you earn more? Take a look at your spending habits. Find something that you do weekly that you could do without. For instance, going to the movies once a week. By the time you pay for the movie for yourself and a companion, buy snacks, pay for the gas to get there, etc, you have spent around $40. This week, instead of going to the movies, rent a video and pop popcorn in the microwave. Rather then spending $40, you will spend only $10, for a total savings of $30. To earn an extra $30, you would have to actually earn $60—half to the government and then half to you. So, by saving money instead of spending it, you actually "earn" double. Thus, a penny saved is two pennies earned.

What does this mean if you are looking to build up your retirement nest egg? It means that you might want to consider saving more as an alternative to earning more. Why work twice as hard?

MILLIONAIRE STORY

Lesson: Be Frugal
Live on "Income" and NOT on "If-Come"

NAME:	Jeffrey
AGE:	76
NET WORTH:	$1.7 million

Jeffrey, a 76 year-old physician had to work until he was 72 before he had enough money to retire. Why?

Jeffrey had to work so long because he and his wife enjoyed living "the good life." He always bought the best cars, took expensive vacations and wore the finest clothes. As a successful physician, he had the income to support his lifestyle.

What Jeffrey didn't do was save much of his income. That is why at age 71 he was still working 12- hour days and treating 35 patients each day in his office.

I don't feel that there is anything wrong with working until your 70's as long as you enjoy it and your health permits.

However, having to work until age 72 in order to save enough for your retirement is not the ideal way to do it. Would it really have been that difficult to save a little more each day? A small reduction in Jeffrey's cost of living would have accelerated his net worth dramatically over the course of a 50-year professional career.

Save more money? How, you may say! How can I ask you to save money when you are saving all you can now? What do I want you to do? Eat less? No, nothing that drastic.

Take a couple of hints from the money-saving methods millionaires I have known. See where they cut back and ways that they saved.

MILLIONAIRES' MONEY-SAVING METHODS

One is Never Enough

Buy in bulk. When you buy in bulk, you save two ways. First, the cost of the jumbo toothpaste is cheaper than the smaller tube sizes. Buying in quantity, for example, by the case, usually gives you a lower bulk rate, too. You also save by buying in bulk because you stay one step ahead of inflation. Buying a case of jumbo-sized toothpaste today that will last you 3 years and will save you inflationary increases in toothpaste during that time period.

I picture many of you shaking your heads and thinking that a few pennies saved in toothpaste is NOT going to build your nest egg up lickety split. The point is to buy in bulk as much as possible, especially when you get discounts or there are sales. Through bulk buying you can have the buying power of $1400 of products while only spending $1000, which, is a 40% savings. And you didn't have to change what you ate at all, let alone eat less!! So, what else can you do?

Shun Plastic

Surely you know that I am going to advise you to pay off your credit cards. This is a must!! Eliminating credit card interest is like earning that money! Think about it this way, if you have $4000 in the bank and $4000 in credit card balances, you are losing money. The money in the bank is earning 2% and the $4000 credit card bill is charging as much as 24%. This means that you are losing 22 cents on every dollar, which is a yearly loss of $840!! Rather than work for your credit cards, make your credit cards work for you. Find cards that pay a rebate or offer frequent flier miles or some other benefit. And NEVER use a card that charges a yearly fee!!

Travel Cheap

Never, I repeat, never pay full price on airline tickets or hotel rooms unless it is an emergency! Several services available on the Internet can get airfares and hotel rooms cheaper than the posted rates. By using orbitz.com, I have stayed in a four star, 2-room hotel suite for 33% of the posted cost. My service was the same, the amenities the same, yet my trip was better because I knew I had saved money! Other money-saving Internet services are available. Just look!

A Car Is a Car

Paying interest on a car loan is like throwing money out the car window. The interest you pay on a car loan, unlike a mortgage loan, does not provide you with a tax deduction. Cars depreciate in value so there is no way to get your money back. You can often find used, economical cars for reasonable prices that don't require loans. If, however, you must finance your car, you might consider a home equity loan. Home equity loans have low interest rates and the interest is tax deductible.

Insurance Is Insurance

Shop around for insurance and buy the one with the most competitive price. Consider the highest deductible you can afford. This will substantially decrease your rates and the savings in premiums will more than pay your deductible over the lifetime of your policy. Be sure to skip any insurance you don't need.

Seniors may reduce the cost of auto insurance by taking an 8-hour AARP sponsored driving class available in communities nationwide.

It's Your Nickel

I wouldn't pay more than five cents a minute on your long distance calls. Plans with monthly fees or specified minutes are often a rip off. Consider getting a cell phone with nationwide free long distance and free weekend calls. For less than $40 per month I have unlimited night and weekend calling and 1000 anytime calling minutes.

Join the Computer Age

Use the Internet to comparison shop. Comparing prices will help you to determine if you are paying the right amount for the things you want.

Save More than Money

Save electricity. Insulation, weather stripping, energy saving light bulbs—they all have the potential to save you up to 35% on your electric bill. Turn down the thermostat in winter and turn it up in the summer for air conditioning.

Don't Get Taken to the Cleaners

Minimize clothes in your wardrobe that require dry cleaning or use the "at home, in the dryer" dry cleaning substitutes. Many people spend over a hundred dollars a month on dry cleaning that could be used to fund their IRAs.

Any Brand Will Do

Buy store brands and you won't be paying for expensive advertising for name-brand items. Store brands are often made by the same companies that make the name brands using identical ingredients. They simply have different labels!

Split the Difference

Often, prescriptions costs can be reduced if you get double strength pills from the pharmacy and cut them in half. For example, a prescription for 40mg Prozac costs less than double the price of a prescription for 20mg Prozac.

Let's say that you are 40 years old and are just beginning a savings plan. After looking over your budget, you feel you can save $400 a month. To become a millionaire by age 65, you will need to double those savings! Although that may seem impossible, by being more careful with your spending it is more than possible and you can do so without drastically changing your lifestyle. All you need to do is look to the millionaires I have interviewed and follow their trails of success.

Look around you. Examine what you do and then see how you can do it more cheaply. Every dollar you save is two dollars you don't need to earn!! And every dollar you save can be used to build your wealth and increase your chances of retiring as a millionaire.

CHAPTER 7

A Word about Debt

Why is there so much month left at the end of the money?
– JOHN BARRYMORE –
ACTOR

Few people become wealthy by acquiring debt. Wealth comes from the disciplined acquisition of savings and investments. In my 20 years as a CPA, I have seen many situations where the modest use of debt assisted the growth of a business. However, personal consumer debt is a different matter altogether. I have never seen a situation in which the acquisition of personal consumer debt was beneficial for anything other than accumulating stress.

The profile of most millionaire retirees is that they have NO DEBT whatsoever.

- No mortgage
- No auto loans
- No credit card balances
- No debt, Period!

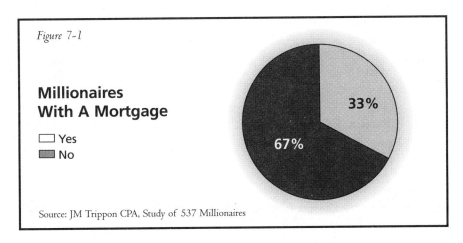

Figure 7-1

Millionaires With A Mortgage

☐ Yes
▨ No

33%

67%

Source: JM Trippon CPA, Study of 537 Millionaires

Most millionaires do not consider the value of a mortgage interest deduction to be worthwhile. The millionaire knows that a deduction for mortgage interest results in saving 28% of your payment, but not having a payment saves 100% of your payment!

MILLIONAIRE STORY

Lesson: Living a Debt Free Life
Drastically accelerate the growth of wealth
and reduce your required cost of living

NAME:	George
AGE:	36
NET WORTH:	$1.3 million

George, a 36 year old physician, became a millionaire in less than 10 years by living below his means and by not having debt. George graduated medical school about 10 years ago. Fortunately, his parents were good savers and valued education, so George did not have any education debt on graduation day.

I met George when he was completing his medical residency. He is a man of integrity and of goals. He sought my advice on how to become a millionaire in 10 years. I told him that given his income, he would have to live a lifestyle that differed from those of most of his colleagues. He would have to spend modestly, incur no consumer debt, and save with discipline.

George accepted the challenge and began to follow my plan. He continued to rent the same condo that he lived in during his training until he saved enough money to buy it with cash. He did not buy a $70,000 sports car. He bought an attractive used car.

He did not accept all the offers for credit cards. He lived modestly but he was neither a miser nor a hermit. George maintained an active social life and took regular vacations. But George did not spend his money foolishly.

Because George was not saddled with debt, he was able to amass substantial savings. As a result of his moderate lifestyle, he also bought his home for cash and in less than ten years became a millionaire. We can all learn a great deal from George.

My advice about debt is simply to avoid it during your retirement. Structure your retirement plan to have no debt whatsoever. If you need help in this area, a resource I recommend is Financial Peace by Dave Ramsey. His course, "Financial Peace University," is also excellent.

If you want to be a millionaire, religiously follow the following four rules:

- Don't have debt.
- Don't use credit cards unless you have discipline to pay off balances in full each month.
- Pay off your mortgage prior to retirement.
- Carry no margin debt on your investments.

The following table shows you the real price of carrying debt.

Figure 7-2	THE TRUE COST OF DEBT		
YOUR 250,000 HOME – TYPICAL 15 YEAR MORTGAGE			
AMOUNT FINANCED	LOAN YEARS	INTEREST RATE	HOME WILL REALLY COST
225,000	15	7.50%	400,440
YOUR 250,000 HOME – TYPICAL 30 YEAR MORTGAGE			
AMOUNT FINANCED	LOAN YEARS	INTEREST RATE	HOME WILL REALLY COST
225,000	30	7.50%	591,363
YOUR $10,000 CREDIT CARD DEBT – assuming 18% interest rate and minumum payment made			
AMOUNT FINANCED	LOAN YEARS	INTEREST RATE	LOAN WILL REALLY COST
10,000	50	18.00%	38,525

CHAPTER 8

Company Retirement and Savings Plans

Money is better than poverty, if only for financial reasons.
– WOODY ALLEN –
DIRECTOR & COMEDIAN

An outstanding way to increase your wealth is by participating in your company's retirement plan. Most large and medium-sized companies provide profit sharing, 401(k) or 403(b) plans for tax deferred retirement savings. These plans provide you with excellent opportunities for easy, tax-deferred investing.

If your company offers such savings plans, take full advantage of them. Your two main goals with company savings or retirement plans should be to contribute the most you possibly can under the plans in order to accumulate greater wealth...in other words, max them out. Since many employers match all or part of the money you contribute to their plans, your failure to contribute is like turning down a raise.

401(K) & 403(B) PLANS

Most companies offer a 401(k) or 403(b) plans (retirement plans) to employees after six months to a year of service. The 401(k) or 403(b) are popular savings plans because many employers match employees' contributions.

> **Simply put, if you don't contribute to these plans, you are forfeiting free money.**

Ideally, you will join these plans at an early age. Why? If you start at age 25, assuming a 10% (percent) rate of return, you only need to contribute

$5.97/day into your 401(k) plan to become a millionaire by age 65. If you wait until age 35 you have to contribute $16.03/day -almost three times as much, assuming a 10% rate of return, so that by age 65 you will have a million dollar balance in your plan.

In addition, 401(k) plans, reduce the amount of federal taxes you will be required to pay. These plans also have the advantage of permitting you to dollar-cost-average your investments. This means that you buy more shares of an investment when the prices are low, and fewer shares when prices are high. Remember however, that dollar cost averaging does not assure a profit and does not protect against loss in declining markets. Since it does involve continuous investments in securities regardless of fluctuating markets, before entering into a dollar cost averaging program, you should consider your willingness to continue purchases during market downturns.

STOCK PURCHASE PLANS

Companies offer Employee Stock Purchase Plans to give employees an opportunity to share in their success . A stock purchase plan enables employees to purchase their company's common stock, often at a discount from the market price. Stock options are perceived by companies to be an effective employee retention and incentive tool. They help employees think more like owners of the corporation because now they have a personal stake in their employer's success.

If employees wish to participate, they indicate the percentages or dollar amounts that they wish to be deducted from their pay during the offering period. The percentages or dollar amounts employees may contribute varies according to each plan. Most plans allow employees to increase or decrease their payroll deduction percentage at any time during the offering period.

Each plan is unique. So read all materials available from your company to get the details on how your company's specific plan works. Company stock purchase plans are described in greater detail in the next chapter.

MILLIONAIRE STORY

Lesson: Maximizing Company Plan Benefits

NAME:	Ron
AGE:	49
NET WORTH:	$2.7 million

Ron believes in not leaving any money on the table. An engineer for a multinational company, he worked on an overseas assignment for five years. Working overseas allowed Ron to qualify for a special incentive bonus plan available only to employees working on foreign assignments. It also allowed him to save virtually his entire salary for five years because the company provided him with both housing and a living allowance. In addition, Ron qualified under a special IRS rule that made a substantial portion of the wages he earned outside of the US tax free.

The net result was that Ron was able to accumulate over $500,000 in savings plus over $50,000 in pension benefits during his five-year overseas assignment. Accepting such lucrative financial opportunities early in one's career can rocket you into accumulating substantial wealth. Those who take advantage of such opportunities can rapidly build up savings that have many years to grow before they retire.

PROFIT SHARING/ MONEY PURCHASE PENSION PLANS

Pension and profit sharing plans are essentially money-saving vehicles established by employers for the benefit of employees. Many different kinds of pension and profit-sharing plans exist, including the following:

Defined Contribution Plans

Examples of defined contribution plans include regular profit-sharing plans, thrift plans, money purchase pension plans, and cash or deferred profit-sharing plans. All of these plans are characterized by the fact that each participant has an individual bookkeeping account under the plan that records the participant's total interest in the plan assets. Monies are contributed or credited in accordance with the rules of the plan established by the employer and contained in the plan documentation. In defined contribution plans, the ultimate amount of funds that are available at retirement depends on how much the employer and employee have contributed, and how much the contributions earned when they were invested.

Defined Benefit Plans

These pension plans base the benefits paid on a formula that guarantees each participant a specified sum per month payable on retirement The amount that each participant is entitled to is calculated according to a predetermined formula that takes into account the participant's age, number of years of service and amount of compensation earned during employment.. Defined benefit plans are not funded individually as are defined contribution plans, but are typically funded on a company-wide basis with equal benefits for all similarly situated employees

Distributions are much more limited in money purchase pension and profit sharing plans than in SIMPLE IRA OR SEP-IRA plans. In order to have access to money in a money purchase pension or profit sharing plan, one of the following must occur:

- Attainment of normal retirement age
- Disability
- Plan termination
- Separation from company service
- Death

See chapters 29 through 31 for more information on taxes and penalties on retirement plan and IRA withdrawals.

Participants' accounts generally must be distributed at age 70 and a half or retirement, whichever comes later.

CHAPTER 9

Company Stock Options

Money isn't everything...
but it ranks right up there with oxygen.

– RITA DAVENPORT –
WRITER & SPEAKER

In addition to providing retirement accounts, companies often provide stock option plans for employees. Traditionally, stock option plans have been used as a way for companies to reward top management and "key" employees and link their interests with those of the company and other shareholders. Increasingly, however, more companies now consider all of their employees "key."

A stock option gives an employee the right to buy a certain number of shares in the company at a fixed price for a certain term of years. The price at which the option is provided is called the "grant" price and is usually the market price at the time the options are granted. Employees who have received stock options hope that the share price rises and that they can "cash in" by exercising (purchasing) the stock at the lower grant price and then selling the stock at the higher current market price. Two principal kinds of stock option programs exist and each has unique rules and tax consequences: non-qualified stock options (NSOs) and incentive stock options (ISOs).

WHAT ARE THE ADVANTAGES TO PARTICIPATING IN A STOCK OPTION PROGRAM?

- They are usually easy and convenient to enroll in (once you are eligible) and encourage saving and investing.

- You generally don't have to commit to a specific number of shares each pay period. You simply select a dollar amount or a percentage of each paycheck and shares are automatically purchased equal to the amount of your contributions.

Incentive Stock Options

Incentive stock options qualify for favorable tax treatment under section 422 of the Internal Revenue Code. They are granted to an employee of a corporation to purchase company stock at a specified price for a specified period of time. Generally, no tax consequences arise until the stock is sold. A qualified plan must meet the following requirements:

- Only employees of the company may participate in the plan.

- The purchase plan must be approved by the shareholders of the company within 12 months of its adoption by the board.

- Any employee owning more than 5% of the company stock may not participate in the plan.

- All eligible employees must be allowed to participate in the plan, although certain categories of employees may be excluded.

- All employees must enjoy the same rights and privileges under the plan, except that the amount of stock that may be purchased may vary on the basis of compensation differences.

- The purchase price may not be less than the lesser of 85% of the fair market value of the stock (1) at the beginning of the offering period, or (2) on the purchase date.

- The maximum offering period can not exceed 27 months unless the purchase price is based solely on the fair market value at time of purchase, in which case the offering period may be as long as five years.

- An employee may not purchase more than $25,000 worth of stock (based on fair market value on the first day of the offering period) for each calendar year in which the offering period is in effect.

Incentive Stock Options (ISOs) enable employees to share in the appreciated value of the stock and provide employers with more flexible arrangements than allowed in qualified retirement plans. ISOs may be designed so that employees may put their capital at risk or to provide them with assistance in financing the exercise price through the use of stock and option exercise programs and employee loan programs. Through ISOs, employees can realize the compensatory gains on the options while employed rather than having to wait until termination of employment.

Nonqualified Stock Options

Nonqualified (nonstatutory) stock options (NSOs) do not qualify for favorable tax treatment under Internal Revenue Code sections 422 or 423. Non-Qualified Purchase Plans are simple payroll deduction plans that allow employees to purchase company stock, often at a discount. Such plans are not necessarily available to all employees.

TAXATION CONSIDERATIONS

Under either type of option (Incentive Stock Options or Nonqualified Stock Options), the employee has the right to buy stock at a price fixed today for a defined number of years, usually 10. When employees choose to buy shares, they are said to "exercise" the option. So if an employee has the right to buy 100 shares of stock at $10 per share for 10 years and if after seven years, the stock hits $30, the employee can then buy the $30 stock for $10.

If the option is an NSO, the employee must immediately pay tax on the $20 difference (called the "spread") at ordinary income tax rates. The company gets a corresponding tax deduction.

With an ISO, the employee pays no tax on exercising the option and the company gets no deduction. If the employee holds the shares for two years after the grant and one year after exercise, the employee only pays capital gains tax on the ultimate difference between the exercise and sale price. If these conditions are not met, then the options are taxed like a non-qualified option. For higher income employees, the tax difference between an ISO and an NSO can be as much 19.6% at the federal level alone, plus the employee has the advantage of deferring tax until the shares are sold.

By offering nonqualified stock options to compensate and provide incentives for employees, employers can give employees tangible rewards for their efforts without expending their liquid cash resources. As a result of such plans, you may get an opportunity to share in the company's future growth.

CHAPTER 10

Portfolio Components

Wealth gotten by vanity shall be diminished:
but he that gathered by labor shall increase.

– PROVERBS 13:11 –

Whether or not an investment program creates substantial wealth or just keeps up with inflation is primarily determined by how the funds are distributed in various portfolio components. For our purposes, "portfolio components" is defined as the asset class in which money is held.

When a client comes to our firm and hires us for financial planning—our first step is always the same regardless of whether the goal is to build substantial wealth for retirement or simply to maintain the wealth they have already created. Our first step is to have the client provide a detailed financial statement that itemizes each and every asset that they own, by account, as well as a listing of all their debts. Typically, this information would be presented to us by our client in a format similar to the following:

Figure 10-1	FINANCIAL INFORMATION AS REPORTED BY CLIENT	
ABC Bank		25,000
Big Bucks Investment Brokerage		135,000
Big Bucks Investment Brokerage – IRA Account		275,000
Employer 401K		1,750,000
Real Estate		500,000
Personal Effects		250,000
	TOTAL	2,935,000

Our job then is to take this information and categorize it in a portfolio component format so that the appropriateness of the client's diversification, investment allocation and earnings capacity for each asset type can be assessed.

The seven portfolio components I use are:

1. Cash

2. Stocks

3. Bonds

4. Real Estate

5. Collectibles

6. Precious Metals

7. Commodities

Many times, a client will only have two or three asset classes in their investment portfolio. However, classifying assets into portfolio components forms the building blocks upon which all strong portfolios must be created.

Let's reexamine the financial statement of the client shown in Figure 10-1. After reorganizing information into the appropriate asset classes, the results would then look something like the following:

Figure 10-2	FINANCIAL INFORMATION AS SORTED BY ASSET CLASS	
Cash		25,000
Stocks		1,450,000
Bonds		710,000
Real Estate — residence		300,000
Real Estate — rental		200,000
Collectibles		95,000
Precious Metals		35,000
Non financial personal assets (furniture/clothing)		120,000
	TOTAL	2,935,000

To assist you in understanding these classes, the definition I use for each category is provided below:

CASH

Cash includes money in your bank account, money in a money market account, commercial paper, treasury bills or money stuffed under the mattress.

EQUITIES

Equities include common stocks, preferred stocks, stock mutual funds and stock index funds.

BONDS

Bonds are essentially an IOU. If the IOU is written by the government it is called a government bond. A bond issued by a corporation that is in good financial condition is considered a blue chip corporate bond. If the IOU is written by a corporation in precarious financial situation, it is called a high yield bond (commonly known in these 1980's as junk bonds.) The common characteristic of most bonds however, is that they usually pay interest.

REAL ESTATE

Your own home is often excluded (not considered as an investment) for purposes in this category. Real estate includes homes, apartments, or raw land as well as commercial investment property.

PRECIOUS METALS

Metals would include gold, silver or platinum.*

COMMODITIES

Examples are pork bellies, orange juice futures, soybeans, as well as different currencies.

* *Note that collectibles are generally not considered as part of your portfolio.*

We need to separately list the types of investments in your portfolio into categories because each asset type has a different risk level and each has a different capacity for earnings and growth. For example, cash in the bank may earn an interest rate of one or two percent, whereas, stocks, historically, have earned as much as eight to twelve percent a year over long periods of time.

Conversely, cash in the bank is advantageous when you need to get your hands on it immediately. At any given point, you know what cash is worth and there is no substantial risk of loss if the funds are in a federally insured bank and the account is under $100,000.00, the FDIC insurance limit.

If you invest money in a stock, it may do well over a long period of time, but in the short run, it may flounder or go down substantially. So, if you needed to sell stock tomorrow, you could face a serious loss .

When examining portfolio components, we do not consider the type of account in which the assets are held. Regardless of whether cash is held inside an individual bank account, an individual brokerage account, a mutual fund money market, an IRA, a ROTH IRA, a 401(k), 403(b), etc, cash is still cash. Portfolio analysis is required in order to break down the portfolio components into subclasses.

For purposes of this book, our focus will be on the three fundamental asset classes generally considered necessary for retirement security:

1. Cash
2. Bonds
3. Stocks

Subsequent chapters will provide more detail on each of these classes. Other commonly used investment types will also be defined, along with brief comments as to their role for the typical millionaire retiree.

CHAPTER II

Cash Reserves

With money in your pocket,
you are wise and you are handsome . . .
and you sing well too.
— YIDDISH PROVERB —

The starting point for your portfolio must be your Cash Reserves. Most of us receive peace of mind by maintaining an emergency fund. However, during your retirement years, the issue of Cash Reserves is a lot more involved than just keeping rainy day money in a coffee can.

I believe your Cash Reserves must be the cornerstone of your investment portfolio. Let me start by defining what I call "Cash Reserves."

CASH RESERVES

Money which you can readily access within 48 hours or less, without a penalty for premature withdrawal, and without risk of investment loss.

Our definition includes moneys in your checking account and passbook savings, but it would also include bank and other money market accounts which offer check writing or instant access. For purposes of this discussion, it does not include certificates of deposit with early withdrawal penalties, bonds or fixed annuities.

Maintaining Cash Reserves as a portfolio component is basic and critical for the following reasons:

I. **Cash Reserves** are the funding source that covers living expenses in retirement. They should be maintained independent of fixed income investments and equities. Interest income and the capital gains from your equities replenish cash reserves after they are spent on living expenses;

2. **Cash Reserves** are your first line of defense that will protect you from being forced into liquidating an equity investment during a temporary market decline;

3. **Cash Reserves** allow you more peace of mind to make long-term investments. With adequate cash reserves you have the luxury of structuring the timing of your purchases and sales to maximize your profits;

4. **Cash Reserves** pay for emergency expenses such as unexpected healthcare needs. However, they are also a reserve to pay for what I call predictable "unpredictable expenses" such as auto repairs, a leaky roof, and your new central air conditioning system; and,

5. **Cash Reserves** give you the option to significantly reduce the cost of your auto, property and health insurance by providing standby reserves so that you can raise insurance policy deductibles.

> **A fundamental shift occurs the day most people begin their retirement. They go from being long-term investors who are always adding to their investments, to retirees who now must draw an income from investment balances.**

Many investment advisors agree that retirees need to maintain Cash Reserves outside their retirement accounts. However, they often take a different position about retirement principal. One belief is that retirement accounts should always be fully invested. The assumption underlying this view is that since cash is assumed to be the lowest performing asset class, it should be kept at a minimum.

This is of course, absolute nonsense! The lowest performing asset class over a short-term period is often a falling stock or equity investment. To illustrate the consequences of this common fallacy, consider the following example:

FORMER MILLIONAIRE STORY

Lesson: Maintain Adequate Cash Reserves

NAME: Jerry
AGE: 60
NET WORTH: $700,000
(formerly 1.1 million)

Jerry retired from a refinery job at the end of 1999, which also happened to be the end of a multi-year bull market. His former investment adviser led him to expect that his retirement accounts (which on the day of his retirement totaled $450,000) could generate a steady income of $45,000 per year because that was the long term rate of return in the stock market according to some table he had consulted.

So Jerry's former advisor invested his entire account into stocks and structured withdrawals for Jerry at the $45,000 annual rate. Here's what actually happened:

	BEGINNING OF YEAR $$$	INVESTMENT INCOME (LOSS)	LESS W/D	END OF YEAR $$$
2000	450,000	(67,500)	(45,000)	337,500
2001	337,500	(50,625)	(45,000)	241,875
2002	241,875	(36,281)	(45,000)	160,594

When I asked Jerry why all of his money had been invested in stocks, Jerry told me that his former broker advised him that "stocks never go down over the long-term." Well, Jerry learned the hard way the significance of that catch phrase "past performance is no guarantee of future results." More importantly, Jerry realized that after you retire not all of your money can be invested for the long term since you need it to pay regular living expenses.

Your cash reserves are your first line of defense that will protect you from being forced into Jerry's situation. Said differently, cash reserves are your insulator that will keep you from having to liquidate an equity investment during a market decline. Therefore, we conclude:

Cash reserves should be maintained both inside and outside of your retirement accounts.

HOW MUCH CASH?

The final question is how much do you need to keep as cash reserves? The answer will vary from person to person and should be discussed with your personal investment advisor. My personal belief is that your cash reserves should cover at least one year of gap needs. What are gap needs?

GAP NEEDS

Gap needs are the difference between your budgeted cost of living expenses and your available pension and social security income. To calculate this amount simply compare:

GAP NEEDS CALCULATOR
YOUR INCOME
1. Retirement Pension Income   _____
2. Social Security Income   _____
3. Total Lines 1 & 2   _____
This is your available income
YOUR EXPENSES
4. Cost of Living (including taxes)   _____
YOUR GAP NEEDS
5. Subtract Line 4 from Line 3   _____
This is your Gap Need

CASH RESERVE SUMMARY POINTS

1. Cash Reserves are the cornerstone of your investment portfolio
2. Cash reserves should be held both inside and outside your retirement accounts.
3. Cash reserves should never be less than 1 year Gap Needs.

CHAPTER 12

Fixed Income

He who gathers money little by little makes it grow.
– PROVERBS 13:11 –

After cash reserves, the next asset in a portfolio is fixed income. Fixed income investments are loans you make to an organization (such as a bank, government agency or corporation) that agrees to repay you with interest. The simplest example is a basic bank savings account. You make a deposit at the bank (i.e. you loan the bank your money) and the bank promises to pay you back your principal along with some interest.

Normally, fixed investment securities are not in the form of savings accounts, but are in the form of bonds. A bond is a loan that you make to the issuer, such as the U.S. government or a major corporation. At the time of maturity, the investor receives the face value of his/her bond. Bonds with that mature in five years or less are called short term bonds. Those that mature in six to 12 years are immediate term and those that run 12 years or longer are called long term.

Fixed income investments play an important role in most retiree portfolios for two reasons. First, they can generate a steady stream of income from which to meet your living expenses. Second, and perhaps more importantly, they can provide a valuable offset to the volatility of equity investments.

Although, over long periods of time, fixed income investments may provide a lower rate of return than stocks, the stability they can provide to your portfolio adds value to your overall finances.

Bonds are one of the primary tools for managing the target risk level in your portfolio: the higher the allocation of the bonds versus equities, generally the lower the portfolio risk. Alternatively, the lower the allocation of the bonds versus equities the higher the portfolio risk.

Fixed income investments do have risks however, including those that can be caused by inflation and opportunity costs, as we will see in the following millionaire story.

MILLIONAIRE STORY

Lesson: Fixed Income Investment Risks

NAME:	Gary
AGE:	54
NET WORTH:	$2.7 million

Gary is a conservative investor when it comes to the stock market, but a very aggressive investor when comes to his own business. Gary has about 2/3 of his wealth tied up in his family run business. The other third, his IRA, is allocated to money market accounts. Gary put his IRA in money market accounts because he is petrified that if he invested it in stocks the market might crash. Fair enough. But Gary had a large portion of his assets tied up in money market accounts during the 1980s and 1990s, which were some of the biggest boom years in stock market history.

What did it cost Gary to keep all his IRA in money market accounts? He suffered no losses in principal. But, his net worth is arguably now much lower than it would have been had he participated in the stock market during those boom years. He and I once ran the numbers. We estimate that had he diversified his portfolio in the 1980's his net worth could have been over double than it is today.

Now let's evaluate a more advanced application, the purchase of a government or corporate bond. In this case, fixed income investing is purchasing a bond that pays a fixed amount of income, which is known as the coupon interest. Coupon interest is usually paid on a semi-annual basis over a set period of time. Most fixed income securities mature in less than 10 years, though the life of some can be substantially longer (in some case up to 100 years.)

Many investors assume that fixed income securities are no-risk investments. Although they typically have lower risk than equity investments, they do carry risks. These risks include interest rate risk, equity risk, default risk, purchasing power risk, call risk and reinvestment risk.

Following is a description of these various types of risk:

INTEREST RATE RISK

Fixed rate securities rise in value when interest rates fall, and fall in value when interest rates rise. Usually, the longer the maturity period, the greater the degree of price volatility. Price fluctuations are known as interest-rate risk or market risk.

EQUITY RISK

Equity risk reflects the value of your investment. It is dependent upon the company's ability to be successful and profitable and the market's ability to recognize that success.

DEFAULT RISK

The risk that a company or individual will be unable to pay the contractual interest or principal on its debt obligations.

PURCHASING POWER RISK

The risk that rising inflation will diminish the rate of real return an investor will realize over time.

CALL RISK

The cash flow risk resulting from the possibility that a callable security will be redeemed before maturity. Callable securities can be redeemed by the company that issued them. This means that the bonds must be returned to the issuer by the bondholder, usually so that the issuer can issue new bonds at a lower interest rate. When a bond is called, the investor is forced to reinvest the principal sooner than expected, usually at a lower interest rate (*reinvestment risk*).

U.S. GOVERNMENT SECURITIES FIXED INCOME

U.S. government securities are the safest bonds in circulation. They are backed directly by the U.S. government or in the case of federal agencies, a moral guarantee, which is described in the section on Federal Land banks below. Most government bonds trade in the secondary or capital market.

U.S. Treasury Bills

Treasury Bills mature in three months or six months and are direct short-term obligations of the U.S. government. T-Bills do not pay interest. They are purchased at a discount. For example, one might buy a $10,000 three-month T-Bill for $9,700. The investor would then receive $10,000 when the T-Bill matures in three months. T-Bills are the only Treasury security issued at a discount. They are also the only Treasury security issued without a stated interest rate. The interest rate is determined at auction. T-Bills are highly liquid.

U.S. Treasury Notes

U.S. Treasury Notes are direct obligations of the U.S. government. They have maturity terms of one to ten years. T-Notes pay interest on a semi-annual basis. T-Notes always expire at par value.

U.S. Treasury Bonds

Treasury Bonds are direct obligations of the U.S. government. They pay interest on a semi-annual basis and mature in 10 to 30 years. 30 year T-Bonds are callable beginning five years prior to maturity.

Federal Land Banks

These loans to farmers and ranchers are supervised by the Farm Credit Association. They are secured by mortgages made by Federal Land Banks through the Federal Land Banks Association. They are not direct obligations of the U.S. government, but are considered moral obligations of the U.S. government. Interest received by investors is free from state and local taxes but not from federal income tax. The income may also be subject to the Alternative Minimum Tax (AMT) for certain investors.

Federal Intermediate Credit Bank (FICB)

The FICB is a group of 12 banks authorized to make loans to farmers. The money loaned is required to be used for farm expenses, machinery, and livestock. The loans may not run for more than 10 years. FICG loans are not direct obligations of the U.S. government, but they are considered moral obligations of the federal government. Interest received by investors is free from state and local taxes but not federal income tax. The income may also be subject to the Alternative Minimum Tax (AMT) for certain investors.

Bank for Cooperatives

The Farm Credit Administration makes loans to farm cooperatives. Interest received by investors is free from state and local taxes, but not federal income tax. The income may also be subject to the Alternative Minimum Tax (AMT) for certain investors.

Federal Home Loan Banks (FHLB)

The Federal Home Loan Bank Board supervises these loan instruments. The FHLB issues debt securities in the open market to loan to FHLB member financial institutions, which in turn, loans this money to their customers to buy homes. Interest received by investors is free from state and local taxes but not federal income tax. The income may also be subject to the Alternative Minimum Tax (AMT) for certain investors.

Federal National Mortgage Association (Fannie Mae)

The purpose of Fannie Mae is to buy and sell real estate mortgages. These mortgages are guaranteed by the Federal Housing Authority (FHA) and the Veterans' Administration. Fannie Mae gets the resources to purchase mortgages from private investors and from borrowing from the Treasury Department. It issues mortgage-backed bonds that can be purchased by investors. Fannie Mae bonds pay semi-annual interest and are regarded as quite safe.

Government National Mortgage Association (GNMA's or Ginnie Mae)

Ginnie Mae, which is wholly owned by the U.S. government, issues 'Modified Pass Through Certificates'. These certificates represent an interest in a pool of mortgages. The pool includes mortgages from the VA, FHA insured mortgages and Farmers Home Administration guaranteed mortgages. As property owners make their mortgage payments, a proportionate share passes through to investors. Payments to investors are paid monthly. The minimum denomination is $25,000. These bonds are backed by the full faith and credit of the U.S. government. The interest is subject to state and local taxes. The income may also be subject to the Alternative Minimum Tax (AMT) for certain investors.

MUNICIPAL BONDS FIXED INCOME

Governmental entities, such as states or local governments issue, Municipal Bonds. These funds support either the governmental entity's general financing needs or are associated with a special project. Municipal bonds are free from federal tax on the accrued interest and are also free from state and local taxes if they are issued in the buyer's state of residence. For example, a resident of New York who buys a municipal bond issued by the state of New York will not be required to pay New York State or local taxes. However, if the same New York resident buys a municipal bond from a city in Connecticut, he/she will be required to pay state and local tax on the accrued interest. Keep in mind that any profit realized from the purchase or sale of municipal bonds is not exempt from tax. Only the accrued interest is tax exempt. The income may also be subject to the Alternative Minimum Tax (AMT) for certain investors.

The different municipal bonds are described on the following page:

General Obligation Bonds (GO's)

General Obligation Bonds are backed by the full faith and credit of the issuer for prompt payment of principal and interest. This guarantee is of an unlimited nature. The issuer can raise taxes as high as they wish to obtain funds to pay these bonds. General Obligation bonds are usually analyzed in terms of the size of the taxable resources. These bonds are generally regarded as a safe investment.

Limited and Special Tax Bonds

These bonds are payable from a pledge of the proceeds against a specific tax. The tax can be a gasoline tax, a special assessment, or an ad valorem tax levied at a fixed price. Unlike General Obligation bonds with their unlimited ability to raise taxes issuers of limited and special tax bonds cannot exceed the amounts that had been set to pay the bonds.

Revenue Bonds

Revenue bonds are payable from the earnings of revenue producing agencies or enterprises. For example water, sewer, school districts, airports, etc. Usually, the yield is higher than that for general obligation bonds, because they have higher risk than GO bonds.

Industrial Revenue Bonds

A local community creates an Industrial Development Agency to develop industrial or commercial property for the benefit of private users. The agency raises revenue to develop the property by issuing municipal bonds. For example, it uses the money raised to pay for construction of the new facilities that are then leased to corporate guarantors. The safety of Industrial Revenue bonds depends on the credit worthiness of the corporate guarantor.

Housing Bonds

Both state and local governments issue Housing Bonds. They are secured by mortgage repayments on single-family homes. Added protections come from federal subsidies for low-income families, FHA insurance, VA guarantees, and private mortgage insurance.

Obligation Bonds

These bonds are issued for a specific purpose (e.g. public housing). It is implied that in the event of a shortfall, the state will make up the difference.

Double Barreled Bonds

They are tax-exempt bonds that are backed by a pledge of two or more sources. Double barrel bonds are similar to general obligation bonds, except they have additional backing by a second source of revenue, which usually increases their safety.

Municipal Notes

Municipal Notes are short-term debt instruments issued by state and local authorities. They usually mature in 60 days to one year and are typically available in denominations of about $25,000. Municipalities use these notes as interim financing in anticipation of future revenue.

Frequently, investors buy long-term bonds because they have higher current yields than short-term bonds. However, be careful. Measure the risk of long-term bonds as an interest-rate risk. Because the price of bonds moves in the opposite direction of interest rates, as interest rates rise, the price of bonds fall.

For example, say you purchase a 20-year treasury bond with a six percent coupon rate. During the next 12 months, interest rates rise two percent, so a new treasury bond is offered with an eight percent coupon. If this occurs, the old 6 percent bonds will be worth less than the new bonds because the new bonds have higher coupons.

The following table illustrates the returns gained from long-term Treasury bond returns from the 1930s through the present.

Figure 12-1	LONG TERM GOVERNMENT BOND RETURNS BY DECADE	
	DECADE	RETURN
	1990s	10.30%
	1980s	12.70%
	1970s	5.50%
	1960s	1.40%
	1950s	-0.10%
	1940s	3.20%
	1930s	4.90%

CD FIXED INCOME

Certificates of Deposit are a good source of fixed income when the stock market is weak, but interest rates are high. However, when the stockmarket is down and interest rates are low, I call CD's Certificates of Depreciation because the interest rates they pay do not keep up with inflation. If CD rates are below the standard inflation rate of 3 to 3.5 percent, you will lose money in the long run. If you look at the cost of living in 1972, the average new car cost $7,600. Now, it's $20,000 and that's not a brand new Lexus or Mercedes. A new home in 1972 cost $38,000 and now the average price is over $150,000.

So there is a potential risk that inflation could rob the purchasing power of your asset. As Senator Alan Cranston once said, "Inflation is not all bad. It has allowed every American to live in a more expensive neighborhood without moving."

The following chapters will further explore equity investments and also how to include fixed income and equity investments in your retirement portfolio.

CHAPTER 13

Equities

*Having more money does not insure happiness.
People with ten million dollars are no happier
than people with nine million dollars.*

– HOBART BROWN –
WRITER

Equities are the final big asset category in a portfolio. Equities differ from bonds because they guarantee no return.

When we speak about equities, we are usually referring to certificates that represent stock ownership in a company. When a new company is formed, the owners (or shareholders) contribute money in exchange for shares of stock, which represent a fractional ownership position in the company.

If the company is already in existence, shares can be purchased from the current owners. When you purchase shares of stock from a stock broker, you are usually purchasing shares that were owned by other investors.

Buying shares of a company's stock gives you direct equity ownership in that company. Any other method of buying equities, such as mutual funds, index funds, options, etc. are called "proxies."

We have all seen the amazing charts that show the long-term benefits of owning equities. Notice how the performance of stocks beats the performance of other investments in the following chart:

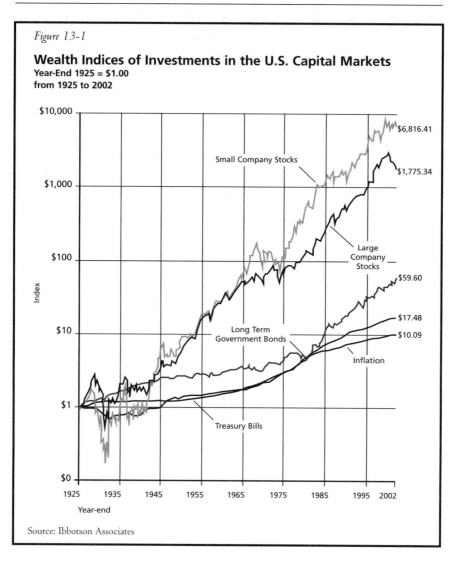

Figure 13-1

Wealth Indices of Investments in the U.S. Capital Markets
Year-End 1925 = $1.00
from 1925 to 2002

Source: Ibbotson Associates

When you examine this chart it makes equity investments look almost risk free, doesn't it? The chart, however, tells only part of the story. If we consider the risk of loss in the stock market in any given year the result can be dramatically different. Notice how heavy the declines in stock prices have been in some recent years:

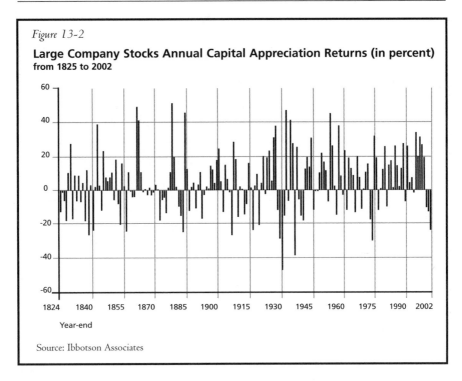

Figure 13-2

Large Company Stocks Annual Capital Appreciation Returns (in percent)
from 1825 to 2002

Year-end

Source: Ibbotson Associates

During a bear market, it becomes painfully apparent to many investors that stocks do not go up in a straight line. In some years, the market is great. While in other years, the market's performance may make you feel like jumping off a tall building without a parachute.

The challenge is to manage the risk of equity volatility during your retirement years, the period when you need a steady and predictable river of income flowing into your bank account.

One of the worst things a retiree can do is to have 100 percent of his/her wealth invested in equities!! Why? Because you cannot afford to be completely exposed to the risks of the market! If you sustain a major stock market loss, your age and living expenses may keep you from ever recovering.

An even greater mistake can be to stay in the market when it is going south!!

SO WHY DO PEOPLE DO IT?

The reasons most people stay invested during a declining market is that either they have been taught to "buy and hold" or that they are afraid of selling only to be left behind when the market rebounds.

These two big fallacies have cost some retired people their fortunes. The financial press tells investors to sit tight, stick with your mutual fund account as it goes from $100,000 down to $20,000. Even after tremendous losses, the talking heads on TV and many advisors tell their clients that buy and hold is always the right approach with equities. I beg to differ!

I am not saying to stay completely away from equities or direct stock ownership. I am saying, however, that you MUST MANAGE YOUR RISKS CAREFULLY...especially if you are retired.

The question is, do we need equities in retirement, and if so, how do you choose appropriate equities for your retirement?

You should consider investing in equities because they provide the greatest potential for return over long periods of time. Look again at Figure 13.1. You can plainly see that over long the long term no other asset class even comes close.

So, how do you select equities? Many investors use mutual funds. A mutual fund is a pooled investment offered only by prospectus that invests according to the objectives of the fund. Your money is commingled with others who ideally have similar investing objectives. The fund's portfolio manager then uses the money to buy investments for the group. The manager can buy stocks in various industries or sectors or may follow an "asset class" approach.

> **Before investing in any mutual fund, you should carefully read the prospectus, which contains complete information including all fees and expenses. Always do this before you invest or send money. I believe the better way to select equities is by investing in asset classes. Although each investor has different goals, tol-**

**erance for risk, varying degrees of investment knowl-
edge and sophistication asset class investing offers a
practical approach for purchasing equities.**

An asset class is a group of securities that share a common systematic risk element. Stocks and bonds perform differently from one another in various market cycles. Small capitalization stocks and large capitalization stocks, domestic and international stocks, and long- and short-maturity bonds all perform differently from one another. Asset class investors believe the difference can be traced to the underlying risk elements of each class. Positioning the asset classes in a portfolio to take advantage of this "diversification effect" is a way to make the portfolio compatible with an investor's risk tolerance and overall goal for rate of return.

Asset class investing is compatible with using either mutual funds or managed accounts with direct ownership of individual securities. Whether you should invest in mutual funds, maintain a privately managed account or some other approach will depend on numerous factors including the size of your accounts and your personal tax situation.

The world's leading academic economists conducted extensive research and found that asset class selection (such as small-cap vs. large-cap, value vs. growth and U.S. vs. international)—not market timing—is the most important determinant of portfolio performance. They discovered that:

1. Markets process information so rapidly when they determine security prices that it is extremely difficult to gain a competitive edge by taking advantage of market anomalies or inefficiencies.

2. Over time, riskier investments provide higher returns as compensation to investors for accepting greater risk.

3. Adding high-risk, low-correlating asset classes to a portfolio can actually reduce volatility and increase expected rates of return. In other words, if some of your assets go up in value while others are decline, you have reduced the fluctuation in your total portfolio and generally have increased the performance of your total investment plan.

4. Passive asset class fund portfolios can be designed to deliver over time the highest expected returns for a chosen level of risk.

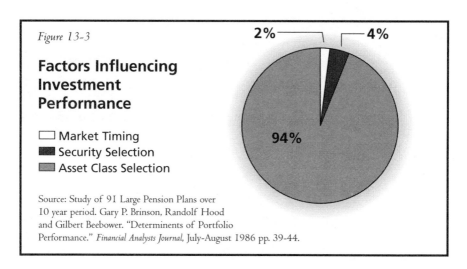

Figure 13-3

Factors Influencing Investment Performance

☐ Market Timing
■ Security Selection
▨ Asset Class Selection

2% 4%

94%

Source: Study of 91 Large Pension Plans over 10 year period. Gary P. Brinson, Randolf Hood and Gilbert Beebower. "Determinents of Portfolio Performance." *Financial Analysts Journal*, July-August 1986 pp. 39-44.

Let's now look at multiple-asset-class investing in a broader equity context. The equity side of the portfolio is usually responsible for great portfolio returns when they occur. The equity side of the portfolio is also most often responsible for significant losses. When seeing the returns of a single asset portfolio versus a two-asset portfolio, most people choose a two-asset portfolio. This is a rational decision since the two-asset-class portfolios generally have less volatility and greater returns than the single-asset-class portfolios. Likewise, the three-asset-class portfolios have better volatility/return characteristics than the two-asset-class portfolios and the four-asset-class portfolios are even better.

If multiple-asset-class investing is so wonderful, why isn't everyone doing it?

REASONS MOST INVESTORS DO NOT USE ASSET CLASS INVESTING

First

Investors lack an awareness of the power of diversification. The typical investor understands that diversification may reduce volatility, but suspects that diversification simultaneously impairs returns. Often, diversification functions to improve returns, not diminish them. Investors need to be educated about this potential dual benefit.

Second

The question of market timing arises. Investors naturally want to believe that there must be some way to predict which asset class will come in first. Some money managers suggest that they can, in fact accurately make such market timing predictions.

Third

Investor psychology. Investors use their domestic market as a frame of reference to evaluate their investment results. For example, a U.S.-based investor will compare his equity returns with a market index like the S&P 500. This form or measurement causes no problems during years when the domestic market underperforms other asset classes, since diversification into better performing markets rewards a multiple-asset-class investor. When the domestic market comes out on top, however, the investor perceives that diversification has impaired his returns.

In the next chapter, we will examine how to construct and manage risk in a portfolio utilizing equity asset classes, fixed income and cash.

CHAPTER 14

Selecting and Evaluating Investments

I'm not concerned about all hell breaking loose,
but that a PART of hell will break loose...
it'll be much harder to detect.

— GEORGE CARLIN —
COMEDIAN

Have you ever browsed in a bookstore for books on investing? The amount of information available is overwhelming and often frightening to anyone who is new to investing.

There are, however, six general rules that will help simplify the process and protect you from many problems.

RULE ONE—DIVERSIFY

We all know that putting our eggs in one basket is not a good move and that diversification is a wise technique for managing investment risk. However, knowing this and doing this are two very different things!! For instance, many people continue to put large amounts of their retirement investments into their former employer's stock.

Why is it important to diversify? The stock market during the year of 2002 provides a perfect example. Stock prices were depressed and, for most investors selling stock would cause a loss. Yet, if all of your assets were in stock and you found yourself in a "cash needing" emergency, you would be forced to take a loss. This would not be true if your holdings were diversified in a way where cash was available.

FORMER MILLIONAIRE STORY

Lesson: Diversify

NAME: Ralph
AGE: 67
NET WORTH: Bankrupt

Ralph, a former millionaire, made a mistake that has been the financial ruin of many former millionaires… he bet everything on his company's stock.

Ralph at one time was worth over $3 million. He had always done well with his company's stock and so by his early sixties he had almost his entire net worth tied up in the common stock of his employer. Bad move! When the company went bankrupt and its stock became worthless, so did Ralph's nest egg.

Think this cannot happen to you? Just ask the retirees from Eastern Airlines, Enron and Global Crossing.

Diversification is not merely owning a couple of dozen different stocks. If these stocks have similar risk factors, such as being in the same asset class or industry, they will move together. Therefore, when one is doing poorly, they all will usually do poorly. Ineffective diversification is illustrated in Figure 14-1.

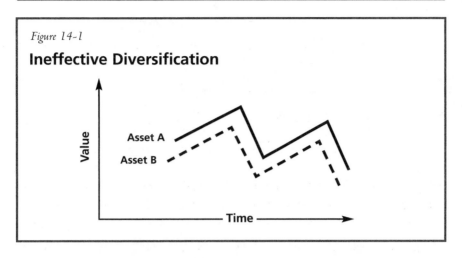

Figure 14-1

Ineffective Diversification

As long as the assets in a portfolio do not move together, you can achieve effective diversification. This point was proven by Harry Markowitz's Nobel-prize winning theory that shows that when the securities in a portfolio do not move together, the risks inherent in each security are reduced. However, please note that diversification does not assure a profit, or protect against loss in a declining market.

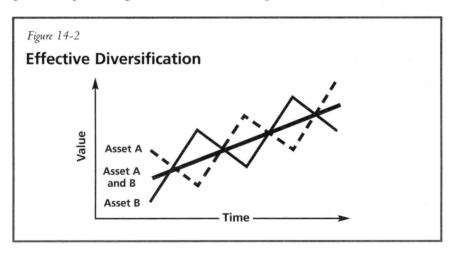

Figure 14-2

Effective Diversification

RULE TWO—THE LESS VOLATILE THE PORTFOLIO, THE HIGHER THE COMPOUND RETURN.

Even if two portfolios have the same average rate of return, the less volatile of the two will produce a higher rate of return. Over time, less volatility increases the probability of a greater compound rate of return. Additionally, reducing the volatile nature of your portfolio will allow you to sleep more comfortably at night and spend a lot less time worrying about your money!! To reduce the volatility of your portfolio, to choose investments that do not move together (as discussed above.) It's impossible to completely remove all volatility, but all reductions in overall portfolio swings can make a big difference in returns.

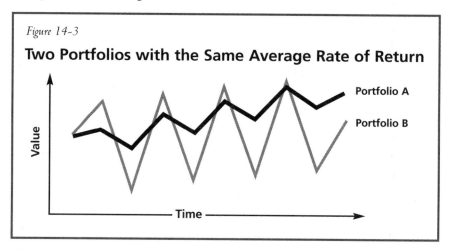

Figure 14-3

Two Portfolios with the Same Average Rate of Return

Portfolio A

Portfolio B

Value

— Time —

RULE THREE—EMPLOY ASSET CLASS INVESTING

Most investment philosophies rely on forecasting the market, which is subjective at best. Investors believe that they can get in when the iron is hot and get out before it turns cold. This type of active management believes that the market is flawed and that predicting where the flaw lies will create wealth. Relying on these philosophies is like trying to get to Hawaii by bus.

The correct tool is asset class investing. It is a more passive management philosophy that believes that the market works. Those who believe in passive investing use asset classes to capture market value. An asset class is a group of securities that have more or less similar risk and return characteristics. Asset-class investing is a disciplined, consistent, long-term approach that is more suitable for planning and reaching financial goals than the speculative "picking and timing" approach. Four important benefits of asset class mutual funds are that they offer

1. low operating costs;

2. low turnover;

3. low trading costs; and,

4. consistent asset allocation.

All mutual funds have operating expenses, including management fees, administrative charges and custody fees. Screening the Morningstar database on December 31, 2002, for the average total operating expense revealed a figure of over 1.50 percent. However, for asset class mutual funds, the average total operating expense is about 1/3 of that cost. An important study by Elton and Gruber in 1993, described in an article in The Society for Financial Studies showed that the worst performing funds were those with the largest expenses. Using asset class mutual funds minimizes this problem.

Active mutual fund managers trade frequently. According to William Harding, an analyst with Morningstar, the recent average turnover rate for managed domestic stock funds is 130 percent.[1] What does this mean? It means that on average, 130 percent of the securities portfolio in a mutual fund have been traded during a 12-month period. Frequent trading is costly to mutual fund owners since each trade incurs transaction costs. And as Elton and Gruber found, large expenses often equal poor performance.

(1)   Source: Mutual fund turnover and taxes, Bankrate.com, March 6, 2002

On the other hand, asset class mutual funds generally have a very low turnover rate of about 25percent. They keep transaction costs low, which may in turn improve returns.

The factor that plays the biggest role in determining performance is how your money is allocated among different asset categories. In many actively managed mutual funds, asset allocations are changed frequently and cash balances are often changed on the basis of market conditions. These changes are made without consideration of your personal situation. Asset class mutual funds, however, consistently maintain their asset allocations, which lower your costs and remain within the risk levels you choose.

In general, asset class investing meets investor needs by reducing risk, allowing you to determine specific risk levels and correlating those risk levels directly to specific asset categories. It also creates a less volatile portfolio with asset classes that do not move in concert with one another. It accomplishes all this with less costs than are typically associated with active management.

The biggest question, though, is: Does asset class investing help investors reach their financial goals? The answer is generally yes. If you use asset class investing, you will not be as tempted to jump on the bandwagon of the latest trends or be influenced to buy the "hottest" new stock. Asset class investing provides a disciplined approach that allows you to focus on long term goals rather than short term noise! The following table assesses the ability to meet investor needs.

Figure 14-4 **INVESTOR NEEDS**		
	YES	NO
Risk Reduction	X	
Return Enhancement	X	
Strategy to Achieve Specific Financial Objectives	X	
Dependable Income Stream	X	
Ability to Liquidate Quickly	X	

RULE FOUR—
GLOBAL DIVERSIFICATION CAN REDUCE RISK

The world equity markets are growing at incredible speed. From 1970 to 2002, they increased over 20 fold, shrinking the US market percentage of the world market as a whole. Looking at world markets is a good way to diversify your portfolio.

Throughout the stock market's history, there have been periods when the United States equity market outperformed foreign markets. During other periods, however, foreign markets outperformed those in the United States. Investing in both US and foreign markets is an often used way to balance a portfolio to take advantage of dissimilar price movements.

Although foreign investment is typically considered more risky than domestic investing, diversifying your portfolio to include both domestic and foreign positions reduces the risk of losses in the market of any one country. Please note however that international investing involves special risks, including currency fluctuations, differing financial accounting standards, and possible political and economic volatility.

There is generally a low correlation between U.S. and foreign markets. And as we learned earlier, a low correlation between markets means less volatility, which translates into higher performance for your investments.

RULE FIVE—DESIGN EFFICIENT PORTFOLIOS

To design efficient portfolios, you must decide which investments you purchase and how much of each you purchase. To determine the optimal combination of asset classes for your portfolio, use the Modern Portfolio Theory. The Modern Portfolio Theory is a mathematical approach that states that for each level of risk there is an optimal combination of investments that provide the best rate of return. Five steps are involved in modern portfolio theory.

USING MODERN PORTFOLIO THEORY

Step One

Determine the expected rate of return for each asset class. Before investing in an asset class, know the expected rate of return so that you can justify your decision to include that asset class in your portfolio. Keep in mind that a higher risk asset class is typically believed to have a higher potential rate of return. (Of course it does not always work out that way.) To determine historical rates, look at the performance of that class for the past 5 years at the minimum. However, tracking it for 10 or more years is preferable. Keep in mind that you must recalculate expected returns on an annual basis.

Step Two

Identify the risk level of each asset class. To find the historical risk of an asset class, look at the standard deviation of the past returns for that class.

Figure 14-5 ASSET CLASS	ANNUALIZED STANDARD DEVIATION
Money Market	3.3%
Two-Year U.S. Government	3.9%
U.S. Large Company Stocks	20.3%
U.S. Small Company Stocks	38.5%
International Large Stocks	20.3%
Emerging Market Stocks	29.0%

Two-Year U.S. Government refers to U.S. Government Bonds and Treasury Bills. These securities are guaranteed by the U.S. government and, if held to maturity, offer a fixed rate of return and guaranteed principal value."

US Large Company Stocks refers to the S&P 500. The S&P 500 is an unmanaged index of 500 widely held stocks that's generally considered representative of the U.S. stock market.

US Small Company Stocks refers to the Russell 2000. The Russell 2000 index is an unmanaged index of small cap securities which generally involve greater risks.

International Large Stocks refers to the EAFE Index. EAFE index is an unmanaged index that is generally considered representative of the international stock market. These international securities involve additional risks including currency fluctuations, differing financial accounting standards, and possible political and economic volatility.

Emerging Market Stocks refers to the MSCI Emerging Markets Free Index. The MSCI Emerging Markets Free (EMF) index is an unmanaged index that tracks 26 country indexes from Asia, Latin American, Eastern Europe, and other emerging markets. These international securities involve additional risks including currency fluctuations, differing financial accounting standards, and possible political and economic volatility.

Step Three

Calculate the correlation coefficients of all the asset classes, which measures the dissimilar price movements among asset classes. Correlation coefficients are measured on a scale from −1.000 to +1.000. The more negative a correlation, the more the movement is dissimilar. For example, if a correlation coefficient is −1.000, then the assets move in opposite directions at the same time. A positive +1.00 value shows that the assets are moving together. Combining asset classes with low correlations will help reduce the volatility of your portfolio.

Step Four

Determine the optimal combination of asset classes for each level of risk. When you have determined steps 1 through 3 above, optimal portfolios can be created. Your objective is to get the highest expected rate of return for each given level of risk. This is graphically illustrated in Figure 14-6:

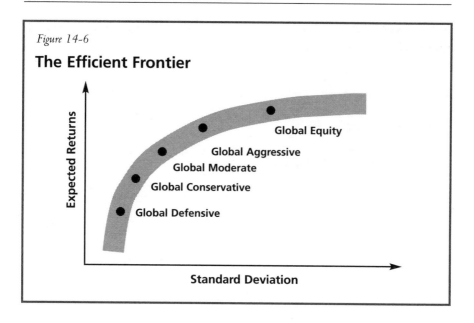

Figure 14-6

The Efficient Frontier

Step Five

Identify your risk tolerance and have your portfolio reflect it.

RULE SIX—MANAGE YOUR EQUITY LOSSES BY USING LIMITS THAT TRIGGER RESTRUCTURING.

Create limits that in a down market will trigger a restructuring of your portfolio. When limits are reached, equities will be pulled out of your portfolio and moved to cash equivalents. Limits could be set to trigger restructuring whenever equities decline to ten percent of their prior valuation. Essentially, the creation of limits is a stop-loss mentality which means that you do not let your losses spiral downwardly while you pray for a magic recovery to save you. Failure to set restructuring limits has destroyed more retirement portfolios than any other factor I have seen during my years as a financial advisor.

Remember setting restructuring limits is easier said than done because there is no way to place stop loss orders on the typical open-ended mutual fund. Accordingly, either you or your advisor must constantly monitor your portfolio performance to avoid potentially devastating losses.

IMPLEMENTING THE SIX
GENERAL RULES TO INVESTING

So how do we implement these rules? The answers differ since everyone has a different tolerance for risk and cost of living structure. Certainly, we want to minimize risk of equity losses, but we also want to stay ahead of inflation.

For the sake of our discussion, let's assume we are attempting to implement the six general rules to a retiree's portfolio. Although everyone's situation and tolerance for risk will be different, and therefore the following allocation is for illustration purposes only, the results of applying the six rules to a sample portfolio might look like this:

Figure 14-7	
ASSET CLASS	ALLOCATION
Cash Equivalents	5%
Fixed Income	50%
Equities	45%
(with varying market sectors & geographic average)	

For the 25 year period from January 1, 1977 through December 31, 2002, the average annual return for US Treasury bills was 6.6%, 12.1% for the S& P 500, and 8.75% for the simulated portfolio.

It is critical for retirement age investors to have a properly diversified portfolio. Being too aggressive is dangerous because the impact of down markets on your principal could be too severe. Being too conservative can also be harmful because inflation and your spending needs can erode your principal.

My advice is to work with a professional who can assist you in structuring an appropriate asset allocation and income portfolio to match your assets and needs.

As you work to create an efficient portfolio, several sources are available to help you evaluate investments.

Your Financial Advisor

Professional experience and advice tailored to your unique situation is critical in structuring an appropriate portfolio.

Morningstar
www.morningstar.com

Provides data on more than 15,000 mutual funds, 8,000 stocks, and 20,000 variable annuity/life sub-accounts worldwide. Products include print publications, software, and Internet solutions.

Value Line
www.valueline.com

Publishes more than a dozen print and electronic products on investment research for stocks, mutual funds, options and convertibles, and offers a family of no-load mutual funds. The company is best known for The Value Line Investment Survey.

Investor's Business Daily (IBD)
www.investors.com

An investment newspaper known for its innovative stock tables. Investor's Business Daily provides information previously available only to pension and mutual funds, banks, insurance companies and government organization.

CHAPTER 15

Your Financial Team

A rich man is nothing but a poor man with money.

— W.C. FIELDS —

ACTOR

WHY HAVE A TEAM?

Why have a team? The answer is simple. It is how most wealthy retirees stay wealthy. The fact is that holding onto wealth is at least as hard as acquiring it. Income and estate tax laws, financial products, investment options, and risk management issues constantly change. Do you really have the time, the interest, and the professional training to keep up with these areas? I thought you were going to spend your retirement time enjoying yourself! In addition, some people get ill and cannot manage their financial affairs.

WHO SHOULD BE ON THE TEAM?

Your financial team should include the following professionals:

1. Comprehensive Financial Advisor

2. CPA

3. Attorney for Wills & Estate Planning

4. Insurance Professional

Often one person can fulfill multiple roles. For example, I am a CPA, as well as a Comprehensive Financial Advisor. If you can find the right person to handle multiples duties then you are fortunate! The professionals that you select for your team should work well together and meet several times a year on your behalf. Let's look at each financial team member and their responsibilities.

COMPREHENSIVE FINANCIAL ADVISOR

Your Comprehensive Financial Advisor is the managing director and quarterback of your financial team. He/she should practice comprehensive planning and not just sell investments. This means he/she will probably not be an old-fashioned style stockbroker. Comprehensive planning includes selecting investments and extends further into the areas of asset protection, cash flow planning, budgeting, tax efficient investing, portfolio maintenance, and risk assessment. This is how most millionaires manage their money as the following chart shows.

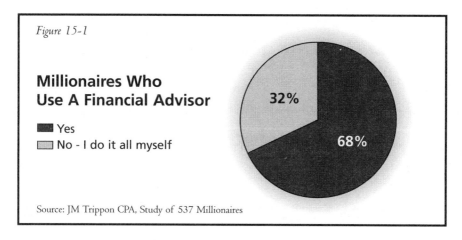

Figure 15-1

Millionaires Who Use A Financial Advisor

■ Yes
▨ No - I do it all myself

32%

68%

Source: JM Trippon CPA, Study of 537 Millionaires

The Comprehensive Financial Advisor is a rare individual in the investment arena. Most investment advisors I have met are primarily focused on selecting and selling investments. That limited focus is counter productive to your financial health and stands in opposition to your need for a long-term advisory relationship.

The litmus test of whether you have the right advisor is to ask if he/she is personally involved in developing plans for his/her clients:

1. Asset Protection:
2. Cash Flow & Budgeting;
3. Tax Reduction; and,
4. Risk Management.

Of course most will say "yes." When they do, ask them for the names of five clients to whom they currently provide these services on a comprehensive basis. If they cannot give you these references, you have the wrong person.

CPA

Taxes are the biggest single expense anyone will experience during their lifetime. They are often also the single biggest expense after death. Therefore, you, and the loved ones who will survive you, need a CPA to help reduce these tax amounts, while working within the confines of exceptionally complex and confusing laws.

ATTORNEY FOR WILLS & ESTATE PLANNING

The simplest way to ensure that after your death, your funds, property, and personal effects will be distributed according to your wishes is to prepare a will. Additionally, you must structure and plan your estate to ensure that the transfer of your assets to your beneficiaries will be quick and have minimal tax consequences.

The process of estate planning includes inventorying your assets and making a will and/or establishing a trust, often with the emphasis on minimizing taxes. Both wills and estate planning require an attorney. Interview candidates to determine their areas of expertise and experience. Then select an attorney who you feel can understand, and represent your interests.

INSURANCE PROFESSIONAL

Many things change throughout our lives: our health, wealth, careers, relationships, interests, etc. A professional insurance agent will assist you in monitoring your changing needs and in protecting your assets. Discuss your need for Long Term Care Insurance, Disability Insurance, 2nd to Die policies, and liability umbrellas for litigation with your agent. Choose an agent who can anticipate your needs through your retirement and has experience in this area. Select one who represents well-established, financially sound company(s) with high ratings.

ASSEMBLING YOUR TEAM

Assembling your financial team involves finding and hiring a group that can work well together. The financial advisor is the most critical position on your financial team. Therefore, we will explore the process of finding the right financial advisor, in greater depth, in our next chapter.

CHAPTER 16

Finding the Right Investment Advisor

If a person gets his attitude toward money straight,
it will help straighten out almost every other area in his life.

– BILLY GRAHAM –
EVANGELIST

MILLIONAIRE STORY

Lesson: Find the Right Investment Advisor

NAME:	Stewart
AGE:	70
NET WORTH:	$1.1 million

Stewart is a retired art dealer whose former financial advisor really did a number on him. The advisor was a product-based advisor, meaning that he was paid commissions on sales but did not provide comprehensive financial planning to his clients. Consequently, Stewart received products from his advisor but not much follow-up on the investments the advisor sold.

The advisor sold Stewart mutual funds with high "back—end" loads which meant that Stewart would be penalized (with exit commissions) if he tried to sell the investments and leave the mutual fund family within the five years of their purchase.

Putting clients into back loaded funds is not unusual and may be appropriate if the advisor does a good job for his client and provides ongoing service. But that's not what happened to Stewart. Unfortunately, his advisor was more interested in finding the next new client than in servicing sales on which he had already made commissions. How did this effect Stewart? When economic events turned and his investments should have been changed, Stewart's advisor was nowhere to be found. The net result is that Stewart suffered over $300,000 in market losses that arguably could have been avoided if the advisor had been involved and on the job.

Choosing an investment advisor is one of the most important steps in getting your financial house in order. An investment advisor will help you set achievable goals and take into account the age you want to retire and the funds that you will require for retirement. The advisor will filter through the endless stream of financial information available and evaluate the products that will enhance your personal situation.

Your first priority should be to find an investment advisor with whom you are comfortable and who meets both your immediate and future needs. A good place to begin is to ask friends for the names of their advisors and if they are satisfied that their financial goals are being met. Also refer to books, check out financial seminars, and read financial newspaper articles to find names of advisors. Most importantly, develop a substantial list of names so that you have several options. Perhaps it would surprise you to know that multi-millionaires often have more than one financial advisor. The following chart comes from my research in this area.

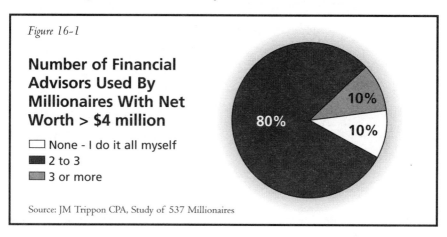

Figure 16-1

Number of Financial Advisors Used By Millionaires With Net Worth > $4 million

☐ None - I do it all myself
■ 2 to 3
▨ 3 or more

Source: JM Trippon CPA, Study of 537 Millionaires

80% 10% 10%

Once you have completed your list, consider the education and reputation of the advisor. What are his/her credentials? How long has he/she been in business? What experience does he/she have with clients in your particular circumstance? Other factors to consider are his/her educational background, recent employment history, current licenses and registrations, with the SEC, a State, or the NASD.

Typically, investment advisors who manage clients' assets of $30 million or more must register with the SEC. If they manage lesser amounts, they normally must register with the state securities agency. Both agencies require the advisor to file a Form ADV, which provides information about the education, licenses, etc. of the advisor and whether there are any problems with a government regulator or a disciplinary history. You have the right to examine both sections of this form.

Additionally, the NASD (www.nasdr.com) was created to regulate the Broker-Dealer profession. NASD's Public Disclosure Program includes information on over 850,000 current and former registered stock brokers and dealers and over 6,000 NASD registered firms. By visiting the NASD site, you can access information on NASD registered advisors and firms within minutes.

Next, go to your list and cross off the name of anyone who does not meet your requirements. Once you are satisfied that an investment advisor has a sound reputation and is properly licensed, consider his/her investment philosophy. Ask whether it matches yours? Before interviewing advisors, try to define your own personal style and develop specific questions related to your financial goals.

Examine what you want. Are you looking for a partner to help manage your investments? Or do you want the advisor to assume primary respon-sibility? Do you have any social or political beliefs that need to be considered? Remember to look for a "teacher" and not a salesman. Find someone who understands the financial buzzwords, and is willing to explain them to you, not just dazzle you with them.

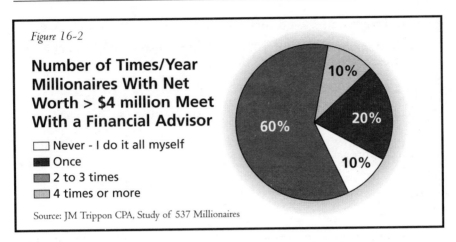

Figure 16-2

Number of Times/Year Millionaires With Net Worth > $4 million Meet With a Financial Advisor

☐ Never - I do it all myself
■ Once
▨ 2 to 3 times
▨ 4 times or more

Source: JM Trippon CPA, Study of 537 Millionaires

Most advisors offer potential clients a no-cost introductory meeting . Such meetings give you an opportunity to determine your comfort level with the advisor both personally and professionally. The following are some questions to broach in your initial interview:

QUESTIONS FOR A
POTENTIAL FINANCIAL ADVISOR

- Will there be an annual review of your strategy or periodic portfolio evaluation?

- How often will we meet?

- What sort of contact can I expect?

- Will the advisor check with me periodically to see if my objectives have changed?

- What products and services are available?

- Does the advisor have access to many different asset classes or just mutual funds?

- Are the advisor's offices conveniently located?

- What are the costs of working with the advisor? Are fees based on a usual hourly rate, flat fee, or commission? Most firms charge a combination of fee based services and commission.

- Will my account be a priority?
- Is the amount of money I intend to have managed comparable to the accounts of their other clients?
- Will the advisor be accessible for questions or for meetings?
- Will other staff members influence decisions made on your account? If so, Get their names and be sure to interview them!

A personal approach to understanding your needs is the cornerstone of a good financial relationship. Good communication is essential and as such it is important for both you and your advisor to identify expectations from the beginning.

The most important ingredient in a successful relationship is chemistry. Chemistry means having mutual trust and respect and reaching a level where you are comfortable and confident in your Investment Advisor's abilities. Trust your heart. If you don't feel comfortable with your advisor, you have the potential to lose more than sleep!

MAINTAINING WEALTH

CHAPTER 17

Four Big Risks

Retirement Day Decisions/Over Withdrawal/Loss of Principal/Taxation

*It requires a great deal of boldness and a great deal of caution
to make a great fortune, and when you have it,
it requires ten times as much skill to keep it.*
— RALPH WALDO EMERSON —
POET

When retirement finances get off track, it is usually for one of four reasons:

1. Retirement day decisions;

2. Over-withdrawal of principal;

3. Loss of principal from investment or unforeseen risks; and,

4. Taxes.

Any of these four areas can create financial loss and keep you from enjoying your retirement. Luckily, with proper planning, all four can be managed properly.

RETIREMENT DAY DECISIONS

The big day has finally come. It is retirement day. You pack the boxes in your office, wave to all your fellow employees and set out to enjoy your new life, right? Well, it depends whether you did your homework.

On the day of your retirement, you will probably be asked to complete forms that will have an enormous impact on the rest of your retired life.

They can include decisions such as:

- Do you want to take a pension annuity or a lump sum payment?
- Do you have medical insurance to cover you now that you are not covered under the employee benefit plan?
- Do you know the tax laws surrounding your 401k, 403b, and company stock plans?"

We will dedicate our next chapter to examining such choices in detail. The key to making successful decisions is finding the proper solution to your unique needs.

Here are some case examples of people who were not completely prepared for the "retirement day" risks. They are real clients, but their names have been changed to protect the innocent (remember *Dragnet?*)

Example 1—Irrevocable Choices

Bob and Betty Jones. Bob knew that he was retiring and had a big smile on his face when he came to see me. He was 63 years old and was retiring from teaching. At the time, the Teachers' Retirement (TR) system offered no option for a lump sum payment. Instead, the TR gave Bob two pension options, and when he chose one it became irrevocable. The choices were:

1. Bob could withdraw $2,600 a month for the rest of his life. When he died, even if it was the day after retirement, his wife, Betty, got nothing.

2. Bob could take a joint pension with Betty, and as long as he lived, Bob would get $2,000 a month pension. When Bob died, Betty would get $1,000 a month in survivor pension benefits.

Bob's initial reaction was to take option 2, the joint pension plan. He cared about Betty and did not want to leave her without income if he died first. Luckily for Bob, he consulted me before making this irrevocable decision.

Take a look at option number two and think about it for a moment. Bob was in a situation where he was going to get $600 less a month for the rest of his life, so that if he died first, Betty would continue to receive money. What do we normally call that? Insurance!! That's not what the TR called it, they called it a different pension option. But in both economic truth and in reality, what they offered was a form of life insurance. If Bob took option 2, he would be paying $600 a month for life insurance for the rest of his life. Although most people choose the married pension option, it may not always be the best financial option!!

I asked Bob these questions: "If you're going to pay $600 a month for the rest of your life for life insurance, how many quotes do you get? Did you only get one quote from your employer or did you see if you could buy it cheaper on your own?"

Bob found that for $400 a month, he could buy enough insurance to leave Betty $2,000 a month for the rest of her life. In this scenario, Bob was better off because he' got a 10 percent higher pension and he paid less for the insurance. Betty is also better off because she will be getting double the pension benefit if Bob predeceases her.

Under the joint pension option, option 2, if Betty died first, Bob would still have to continue to pay $600 a month for the insurance. Remember, I said it was an *irrevocable election*. So, he would be paying $600 for life insurance that no one can ever collect since there is no surviving beneficiary. That wouldn't make a lot of sense!

Example 2—Tax Rate Options

John and Mary Smith. John is 67 years old and lives in suburban Houston. John was planning to take $250,000 out of his pension account for two reasons. First, because he wanted a vacation home and second, because he wanted a new boat.

Under the normal tax rates, after factoring in his salary and the lump sum payout, John, who filed a joint return, would pay roughly $95,400 in taxes to get that $250,000. Out of the $250,000, he would have ended up with only about $150,000. But because John worked for a company that included stock as part of his pension plan, John might have used a special capital gains rate election which would have cut his tax in half. We will get more into this in chapter 30—but the point is that John could have received a substantial tax reduction had he simply checked out the differing tax rate options before making his irrevocable decision to take a lump sum withdrawal.

Example 3—Timing Pension Withdrawals

Bill and Donna Ford. Bill was 66 when he came to see me and said he was planning to retire in a year. He had $200,000 in his 401(k) account that he didn't need immediate access to because he was going to continue to work as a consultant for another ten years. How should Bill handle his money when he retires?

Bill has four choices. He can:

1. Withdraw his 401k money now and pay tax on it now.

2. Withdraw the money now and rollover the net money he receives (after factoring a 20% federal withholding rate) into a new rollover IRA.

3. Rollover the money directly from the 401k into a new rollover IRA.

4. Do nothing now and either withdraw or rollover the money at a later date.

Bill's best moves for income tax purposes would be either option 3 or 4. If he chooses option 1 or 2 Bill will pay unnecessary taxes. With options 3 or 4 Bill will pay no tax on the day he retires and maintain maximum flexibility for the future.

WHAT'S THE MORAL OF THESE STORIES?

Get professional investment advice.
Everybody's situation is different.

THE PROBLEMS OF OVER WITHDRAWAL

One of the biggest fears during retirement is running out of money. One of the fastest ways to do this is by over withdrawing your accounts!!

If you take out more money than your investments earn, you will soon dip into your principal and the never-ending downward spiral will begin.

The stock market decline that started in the fourth quarter 1999 had by mid-year 2002 taken a severe toll on many people seeking my investment advice. Let me share with you Jim's story.

Jim retired from an oil company in 1999. Jim took early retirement at age 55 and he wasn't ready to stop working. Friends who had retired early teased him about what he was missing! "You're young and healthy," they told him; "You should you be traveling the world and enjoying yourself." Of course, the fact that in the late 1990's people commonly made over 15% a year on their investments, gave them the false security that it would last for ever.

During this period, while the market enjoyed one of the biggest bull upswings in history, Jim's friends made more money from the increase in their retirement portfolios than they ever made working. They told Jim he could do the same and he believed them.

And so Jim retired. He took his retirement accounts, which amounted to over $400,000, to a well know brokerage firm. The brokerage firm put the money into a "moderate risk" diversified portfolio. His portfolio was invested in categories with names like "Blue Chip" and "Large Company". He could withdraw 10% a year and never "have a worry," they assured him.

Jim felt safe. He wanted to enjoy all the things his friends were savoring. He wanted to spend more time with his family.

At first, he didn't notice a problem. His broker established an IRS rule 72t distribution from his IRA, which meant that he would receive a steady income of $3,625 each month. Under the provisions of IRS rule 72t, in order to receive distributions from an IRA account before age 59 fi, a retiree must agree to withdraw equal amounts for at least the first 5 years of his retirement. If any change is made to the withdrawal, the retiree is subject to a 10% penalty on all amounts withdrawn.

So Jim began receiving monthly withdrawals . He first became concerned when he received his 1999- year end statement and he noticed his "diversified portfolio" had been falling like a rock. The decline continued throughout both 2000 and 2001, at which point their financial worries were giving Jim and his wife sleepless nights.

When Jim first consulted with me, his $400,000 retirement fund had crashed to approximately $163,000. He had gone back to work full time because at the rate his IRA was declining, he would have run out of money in less than five years. He wanted to know what advice I had for him. The advice I gave him is the same I have for you.

Never set up a withdrawal program that exceeds a reasonable average earnings capacity rate of return for your portfolio.

LOSS OF PRINCIPAL
FROM UNFORESEEN RISKS

Unforeseen risks? Like what? How about liability suits for events that occurred before you retired or other general litigation? You could also incur debts as a result of remarriage, scams and swindles, fees and commission, and unexpected healthcare problems. Any of these can eat into your principle and cause you to end up broke.

Take Jenny, for example. Jenny, a spirited and independent lady, has been married to Joe for over 60 years. About seventeen years ago, Joe's health and memory started to decline and Jenny realized that Joe needed more and more assistance. So Jenny took Joe for a checkup and learned that Joe was in the early stages of Alzheimer's disease. Eventually, Joe's conditioned worsened to the point that he required around-the-clock care that (although it broke Jenny's heart) meant Joe had to move into a nursing home.

At first, Joe's confinement did not place too much of a financial burden on Jenny because she and Joe had always been savers. They had substantial ready cash savings as well as almost a million dollars in the stock market. Fortunately, the stock market was going up and Jenny did fine for quite some time.

During the next few years, Joe's condition worsened, and the cost of his care mounted . Jenny had to maintain her own residence and fund Joe's around-the-clock care. After five years Jenny exhausted her ready cash and began withdrawals from her stock market investment fund principal.

After ten years of care, Joe was still in the nursing home and Jenny had eroded about one third of her investment fund principal. Now, some seventeen years since Joe began receiving long-term care, Jenny is about three years away from being flat broke. At this point, she can do nothing except wait for the inevitable day when her money runs out.

Could this have been prevented? Jenny and Joe could have bought long term care insurance to cover the expenses that Medicare didn't cover. Had they done so, Jenny could have maintained both her financial security and the dignity of being financially independent.

TAXATION

Our tax laws are unbelievable at best and impossible at worst!! Before saying much more, I want to stress that you should get good advice from a CPA. Having someone on your side who knows the tax laws can substantially increase your spending power.

Let me give you an example of how ignorance was not bliss. A woman who attended one of my workshops, took some of her retirement money and invested it in the bank. When she turned 70-1/2, she didn't take the required governmental withdrawal. Why? Because she didn't know she had to. She first learned of this requirement when the IRS sent her a notice saying, "Please send us 50 percent of what you were supposed to withdraw as a penalty for not doing so." In addition to the 50 percent penalty, the IRS began charging her late payment penalties and interest at a 60 percent rate compounded daily. You certainly don't want to get into that situation!!

The following chapters deal with each of these issues. And an entire section is devoted to taxation.

CHAPTER 18

Your Retirement Day
Decisions for Forever

From birth to age 18, a girl needs good parents,
from 18 to 35 she needs good looks,
from 35 to 55 she needs a good personality,
and from 55 on she needs cash.

– SOPHIE TUCKER –
SINGER

If you work for a company with traditional pension or health insurance benefits your retirement day is an important one. This chapter will explain the typical decisions made at retirement.

On your retirement day, your employer will probably ask you to provide written instructions on how to handle your pension and other benefit plans. The critical point is that the decisions you make on retirement day are usually *irrevocable*. Once you make your retirement choices with your company, you will probably have to live with them for the rest of your life.

Therefore, the starting point for your retirement day decisions is to

- First, know all of your options. Start by obtaining a copy of your company benefit plan. Most employers routinely distribute this information in written or Internet form.

- Second, request sample copies of the retirement election forms so that you can review them, in relation to the written benefit policies, with your CPA and financial team.

YOUR DECISIONS

Often, your first decision will be how to handle any company funded retirement plans. Your choices generally fall into two basic categories: taking either

1. a lifetime annuity pension or
2. a lump-sum, one-time buyout.

Annuity Pension

An annuity pension is a lifetime monthly payment which will be paid only as long as you live. The monthly amount you receive is generally not increased by inflation adjustments if the cost of living changes in the future. This also means that the first monthly amount you receive upon retirement will be the exact amount you get on the last month of your retirement—even if the cost of living has soared.

Another consequence of accepting a lifetime pension is that if you die the day after your retirement begins, the company has no further pension obligation to your heirs. To offset the drastic impact your death might cause, most companies offer either spousal continuation rights (at a reduced monthly pension amount) or a period certain option (also at a reduced monthly pension amount). They provide that benefits will be paid to your spouse for at least a minimum fixed number of years if you die within a set time. (If your spouse dies prior to the expiration of the fixed term, the remainder of the benefits for the period certain would be paid to your heirs.)

Once you start taking pension payments, you cannot switch to a lump-sum buyout. You will continue to receive monthly payments and pay taxes on them. The money you receive is not eligible for IRA rollovers, even if you take another job and are no longer "retired."

Another major issue is a risk of loss in the event your company fails. Let me share a "former millionaire" story with you that provides an chilling example.

FORMER MILLIONAIRE STORY

Lesson: Retirement Decisions Have Long-Term Consequences

NAME:	Ralph
AGE:	80
NET WORTH:	$200,000

(previously 1.4 million)

One of my very first clients twenty years ago was a commercial airline pilot who worked for Eastern Airlines. Do you remember what happened to Eastern Airlines? It went bankrupt.

Before Eastern went under, my client retired and started receiving his pension. Later, when the company went bankrupt, he was almost wiped out. The reason was that one of the main assets in both the company pension plan and my client's portfolio was Eastern Airline stock. Like many retirees, Ralph was emotionally attached to his former employers stock and would not sell it to diversify. When the company failed, its stock became worthless, which had the following consequences on Ralph's finances:

1. It reduced Eastern's ability to make its pension payments to Ralph.

2. It crushed the value of Ralph's personal investment portfolio which had been heavily invested in the airline.

3. It forced Ralph to withdraw principal from his IRA in order to pay his living costs. Depleting his principal will eventually wipe out Ralph's remaining money unless he goes back to work or lives a Spartan life.

The lesson here is that decisions on retirement day (such as Ralph's decisions to hold most of his wealth in one company's stock and collect a pension instead

of taking a lump sum rollover in cash) can have long-term consequences.

You may be wondering if the government steps in to help retirees of bankrupt companies. Did Ralph lose his entire pension? No, he did not, because the government provides pension guarantees through the Pension Benefit Guaranty Corp. which works similarly to the F.D.I.C.

If you had money in the bank and the bank fails, does the F.D.I.C. protect you? Only if you have less than $100,000. If you have more than $100,000 in the bank, then depending on your account registrations, you may not get all your money back. The same concept apllies to pensions with the Pension Benefit Guaranty Corp. In this case, when Eastern Airlines failed, Ralph did not lose everything. Ralph only lost about 60 percent of his pension along with a substantial portion of his IRA and stock portfolio, which he had invested in Eastern Airlines stock.

I'm sure we will see similar situations with employees of other big companies that fail. The employees may not get all their pensions and that is one of the major factors to consider when making the decision to take an annuity versus a lump sum payment.

Lump-Sum (One-Time Buyout)

Many companies offer a lump sum option as an alternative to a life pension annuity. A lump sum buyout is a single payment made by a company in lieu of a lifetime of monthly pension annuity benefits. The amount retirees receive is calculated on life expectancy and interest rate assumptions, which may vary from company to company.

If you take the lump sum option and invest well, your monthly income may be significantly higher than if you took the monthly pension annuity. On the other hand, if you take a lump sum and suffer investment losses, you will receive no additional income from the company because the company has met it's obligation to you.

So, the decision is not really as simple as annuity versus lump sum. You also must decide whether you want the dollars paid out over your lifetime or have them paid jointly to you and your spouse. Joint payments may provide income for your spouse in the event you die.

Get professional advice if you are offered a choice between a lump sum payout and a lifetime annuity pension . I believe that in many cases a lump sum can be the better choice.

FIVE REASONS I BELIEVE LUMP SUM IS GENERALLY THE BEST CHOICE

1. **Inflation**

   Historically, the inflation rate in the United States runs between two to three-and-a-half percent. If you retire from most companies, you will receive the same pension amount in dollars thirty years from now that you get today. The problem is that thirty years from now, goods and services will be a lot more expensive. To illustrate this fact, look at postage. Thirty years ago a postage stamp cost 9 cents and now it costs over four times as much. If you take a fixed pension annuity, you have no hedge against inflation.

2. **Emergency Cash Reserve**

   If you have a medical or family emergency and need to get your hands on some money, an annuity does not provide you with access to a large sum of money. If you take a lump sum and roll it over into an IRA, you will have access to withdraw whatever you want from the IRA.

3. **Flexibility of Income Payments**

   If you retire and then decide to go back to work, you have the option to stop the income so you don't have to pay tax on it until you need it.

4. **Controlling Your Investments**

   Receiving a lump sum payment allows you to make investment decisions, which can be good or bad, depending upon your ability!!

5. Money for Survivors

Once you die, a lifetime annuity stops. If you instead take a lump sum, then the money could be rolled over to your children and in fact, it can be rolled over in tax efficient ways.

The following chart summarizes the pros and cons of each retirement fund option.

Figure 18-1	COMPARISON OF LUMP SUM VS. LIFETIME PENSION ANNUITY	
	LUMP SUM	LIFETIME PENSION ANNUITY
Protection Against Inflation	Yes	No
Emergency Withdrawals Available	Yes	No
Flexibility on Tax Recognition	Yes	No
Control of Investments	Yes	No
Money for Survivors	Yes	No
Guaranteed Monthly Return	No	Yes

If you choose a lump sum payment, how do you manage it? One option is a self-directed IRA because it gives you control of your own investments. There are some penalties you should be aware of that are becoming bigger issues because people are retiring increasingly earlier.

IRA PENALTIES

If you take money from your pension, roll it over to an IRA, and then withdraw it before age 59 and a half, you will be subject to a 10 percent early withdrawal penalty . (That's different than if you left your money with the company. If, after you are age 55, you leave your money at the company you can withdraw it without penalty until age 59 and a half and then you can roll it over.)

So, in light of these penalties, what are the consequences for you? The general rules are that:

- If you are younger than age 55, you probably should not leave your money at the company.

- If you are older than 59 and a half, you probably should not leave it at the company in a 401k account.

- If you are between 55 and 59 and a half, you may want to leave some money in the company retirement plan because you can withdraw it within those 4 and a half years without paying any tax penalties.

For estate planning purposes, it is generally not a good idea to leave money in your company plan after you retire. If you died and the money was left to anyone other than a surviving spouse, such as a child or a grandchild, the entire amount could become fully taxable in the year of your death. Taxes would cost your beneficiaries 40 to 70% and even more if your surviving spouse is not a United States citizen.

HEALTH INSURANCE AND MEDICARE

If you are retiring at age 65, Medicare will normally cover your basic medical insurance. It does not cover all of your medical expenses, as we will discuss in a later chapter. Because Medicare will not cover all of your expenses, I am a strong believer in the use of Medicare supplement insurance. This insurance covers the portion of healthcare costs not paid by Medicare. Consult your insurance agent about the details and options for this type of insurance.

- If you retire before age 65 you will be responsible for your own health insurance coverage until you become eligible for Medicare.

- If you are under age 65, be sure to determine whether your employer offers any form of medical coverage for retirees. If retiree coverage is not offered, begin to search for gap coverage early. Bear in mind, that it might take several weeks to locate coverage outside of your employer. Also remember that you may be eligible for coverage under the *Consolidated Omnibus Budget Reconciliation Act* (commonly known as COBRA) for up to 18 months after retiring.

LIFE INSURANCE

Many employers offer to continue your life insurance benefits (for a premium that you pay) after the date of your retirement. Continuing coverage might be a good idea if you need coverage or are uninsurable. If you decide to elect this option, be sure to compare prices with policies that you can buy directly on your own. Also, consider having the policy or certificate of coverage held by a tax avoidance trust as discussed in the estate planning section in Chapter 40.

COMPANY STOCK IN BENEFIT PLANS

The NUA Advantage

One of the most lucrative tax loopholes that you can take advantage of at the time of your retirement is called the "NUA (Net Unrealized Appreciation) advantage." Net unrealized appreciation is the gain in value in your company stock from the time it was first purchased until retirement occurs.

Many employers offer Company stock to employees for purchase through the company 401k, profit sharing, or another retirement plan. If you have bought company stock in this manner, the value has probably increased substantially and you might be eligible for the NUA advantage.

The top tax rate on rollovers to an IRA that you subsequently withdraw is approximately 40 percent. However, if you qualify for the special election available for withdrawal of stock certificates from a company retirement plan (the NUA advantage), you may be able to pay a 15 percent tax rate or less than half the top rate. Unless you like funding the government, this special election is an option worth investigating!

Since the NUA advantage is an advanced planning technique, I have dedicated all of Chapter 30 to it. The bottom line is that company stock in your retirement accounts, may qualify for substantial legal tax loopholes that lower your taxes for the rest of your life. Get professional advice before retirement because once you retire, it is too late to try to take the NUA advantage.

CHAPTER 19

Withdrawal Strategies
Applied Budgeting

Money is a terrible master, but an excellent servant.

– P.T. BARNUM –

SHOWMAN

One of the most difficult situations I see as a financial advisor is when retirees are forced back to work because they have made excessive withdrawals or suffered losses to their retirement investment portfolios.

In this chapter we will look at strategies to avoid getting into this situation. We will also explore how to determine appropriate withdrawal rates from retirement savings.

Let's assume you want to develop a strategy for income in retirement and have a portfolio that consists of the following:

Figure 19-1 ASSETS	PORTFOLIO %	ESTIMATED LONG-TERM RATE OF RETURN
Cash/Money Markets	20%	2%
Fixed Income/Bonds	40%	6%
Equities	40%	8%

We would first calculate your average estimated earnings capacity rate as follows:

Total estimated earnings capacity   7.0%

In this case, the estimated withdrawal rate from savings and investments should not exceed 7%.

Remember Jim from Chapter 17? His $400,000 investment portfolio dwindled to just over $150,000 in 3 years. His former advisor made three fundamental mistakes:

WITHDRAWAL MISTAKES

1. Withdrawals were set a rate that exceeded the reasonable earnings capacity of his holdings.

2. Inadequate amounts were held in cash and fixed income, which exposed Jim's entire retirement savings to wide declines in value as the stock market declined. (This is the same as saying there really was no diversification.)

3. No risk management tools, such stop losses, were used. I recommend the consideration of stop losses at a 7% to 10% level for retirement portfolios.

The combination of the three errors above resulted in Jim losing 60% of his portfolio. Of course, there is no guarantee that had Jim followed the program I outlined, he would have earned 7% on his portfolio during the same period. In fact, it is quite likely that Jim would have still suffered a loss in the value of his portfolio. But he would not have experienced anywhere near the financial devastation that occurred.

HOW CAN I SAY THAT?

Well, I ran hypothetical numbers on Jim's portfolio assuming that he followed my earnings capacity withdrawal methodology (using 7% as a withdrawal rate). I also assumed that he originally diversified his portfolio into 20% cash, 40% stocks and 40% bonds. I calculated that Jim used a stop losses order that was triggered at a 7% decline level and I assumed that he was stopped out at those amounts.

WHAT HAPPENED TO JIM WITH MY APPROACH?

Well, Jim still lost money. But, under my methods, he would have experienced a hypothetical market loss of only 14.7% instead of his actual 60% loss. He might not have been forced to go back to work fulltime.

However, I've got good news for Jim. By applying the portfolio allocation methodology explained in chapter 14, all is not lost. Jim's recent return to fulltime work, together with a more appropriate portfolio will likely allow his finances to recover in time. Under our current projections he will be able to retire at age 65.

WITHDRAWL LESSONS TO BE LEARNED

First

Be sure to calculate and apply the reasonable earnings capacity of different asset classes.

Second

Be extremely careful when utilizing a rule 72t withdrawal program. If you should over withdraw, you risk running out of money and suffering significant tax penalties.

CHAPTER 20

Catastrophic Personal Expenses

How to Avoid Running Out of Money During Retirement

You can be young without money,
but you can't be old without it.

– TENNESSEE WILLIAMS –
WRITER

Whoever said that ignorance is bliss, has never had to advise someone who has lost their life savings due to an unexpected catastrophic personal expense.

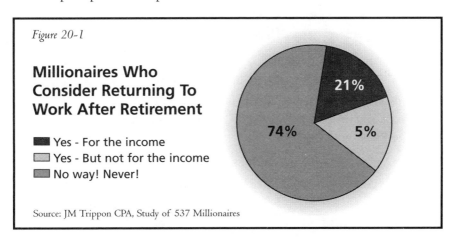

Figure 20-1

Millionaires Who Consider Returning To Work After Retirement

■ Yes - For the income
▨ Yes - But not for the income
▥ No way! Never!

21%
5%
74%

Source: JM Trippon CPA, Study of 537 Millionaires

For over five years, I have taught retirement workshops to retirees and prospective retirees. In the weeks following these workshops, I have met individually with people who are exploring the possibility of having my firm manage their retirement assets.

You would probably not believe me if I told you some of the events that caused people to lose their fortunes. "Truth is often stranger than fiction", as I have personally observed on more than one occasion. There seems to be an apparent pattern to these events, which for some unknown reason recurs time and again.

The most common unexpected catastrophic expenses I have seen are listed below in order of frequency.

COMMON CATASTROPHES

1. Unplanned Healthcare Expenses

2. Investment Scams & Swindles

3. Debts Acquired in Remarriage

4. Unplanned General Litigation

5. Professional Liability Law Suits for Events that Occurred before Retirement.

The first three events occur so often that I have written individual chapters to address each of them. This chapter will focus on the last two conditions, namely, litigation expenses from unplanned general liabilities and litigation expenses from pre-retirement career related activities.

Have you ever watched late night television and seen an advertisement for some "gunslinger" trial attorney? You know, the ones who want you to call their toll free 800 numbers if you have been injured in an automobile accident.

Most of us have seen those ads and perhaps wondered how they can afford to spend so much money on advertising. I used to wonder also, especially when I was hired by one of those attorneys to do his CPA work and noticed that his two-man law office spent over $40,000 a month on TV advertising.

The mystery was quickly solved when the attorney explained how much money could be made off the "right case." There are times when law firms are paid as much as a million dollars in fees for a single client. Where does this money come from? It can come from you, if you are the unfortunate target of one of these lawsuits!

Let me share a "former millionaire" story with you:

FORMER MILLIONAIRE STORY

Lesson: Plan for Litigation and Have Adequate Insurance

NAME: Susan
AGE: 58
NET WORTH: Approx. $275,000
(previously $2.4 million)

Susan was a multi millionaire and a successful business owner. She had worked years to build a business that helped people and made a predictable profit. But she never planned for litigation, which can be a fatal mistake in this world we live in.

One day, Susan got in a dispute with an employee who she felt was stealing. Susan fired the employee and the employee filed a lawsuit against Susan and her company for what the employee claimed was a wrongful termination because of "discrimination."

A jury awarded the employee over a million dollars for her claims against Susan, who they viewed as a "rich business owner."

The result was that both Susan and her business went bankrupt and Susan lost almost everything.

A reasonable litigation plan and liability insurance could prevented the law suit from wiping Susan out.

Likewise, I also work with retired physicians who have been sued by their former patient's years after they retired .

WHAT CAN YOU DO ABOUT IT?

I recommend three steps:

1. Maintain a general liability insurance policy (sometimes just called an "umbrella" policy). The policy should be for a minimum of $1 million in coverage. Call your agent to determine the proper coverage for your situation. You will find it very inexpensive considering the alternative.

2. If you retired (or will be retiring) from a profession that is commonly sued, such as a physician or an attorney, I recommend that you purchase a special type of professional liability insurance called "tail coverage." Tail coverage is the insurance that will cover you after you retire, for lawsuits regarding events that happened prior to retirement. See your agent for details.

3. I also recommend that you consider purchasing a "pre-paid legal" services policy. In many cases it is not the ultimate settlement that is financially devastating, but the cost of legal representation. These types of policies can reduce your exposure to the cost of litigation.

Doing these three things can significantly reduce your risk of loss in this area.

CHAPTER 21

Healthcare Expense Risk Management

Money is plentiful for those who understand
the simple laws which govern its acquisition.
—GEORGE S. CLASON—
PUBLISHER & WRITER

Do you know what the number one cause of poverty is in the United States for people over age 65? I often ask this question when I am teaching a workshop to potential retirees and the answers I get range from the flippant "not having enough money" to the vague (but more accurate) "unexpected expenses."

Actually, the number one cause of poverty for people over age 65 is unplanned health care expenses. The next three chapters will help explain healthcare costs, and possible solutions to managing them. These unplanned health expenses fall into four categories:

1. Hospitalization Costs

2. Prescription Drug Costs

3. Physician's Fees

4. Long-term Care Costs

Many people assume that when they reach age 65 Medicare will pay all of their healthcare expenses. This isn't true. In fact, the portion of hospitalization, prescription drugs and physicians' expenses not covered by Medicare costs some retirees thousands of dollars per month. Even more problematic is the area of long-term healthcare. In most cases, Medicare will not pay for any of the costs associated with long-term care.

Let's start by reviewing what Medicare is and isn't. Medicare is a federal health insurance plan available to most Americans over age 65, and to some disabled individuals under age 65. Medicare consists of two parts, Part A and Part B.

Part A of Medicare covers hospitalization, skilled nursing care, home health, and hospice services. Part B of Medicare covers physician fees, X-rays, lab tests and ambulance services. Both Part A and Part B have deductibles and co-insurance provisions that can leave you exposed to thousands of dollars of uncovered costs. These uncovered costs hurt worst in the areas of prescription drugs and long-term care.

What is long-term care? Long-term care is assistance provided to enable patients to conduct the activities of daily living, which they may be unable to handle because of declining health. If injury or advanced age prevents you from conducting daily activities such as dressing, bathing, walking, etc., you may need to hire someone to assist you.

When this assistance is provided in your home it is called "at-home long-term care". If this assistance is received in a residential facility other than your home, it is referred to as "assisted living" or "nursing home care." The main point is that it is unlikely that Medicare will pay the expenses you incur if you need this type of healthcare. If you are indigent, you may be able to obtain coverage under Medicaid. However, becoming a Medicaid recipient is not a financial goal of choice, but rather of last resort.

As I have said, the most devastating unplanned health care costs are expenses for long-term care. The reason that long term care is so devastating is that it can double the living expenses for a retired couple.

According to an AARP study, the average cost of a one-year nursing home stay during 2001 was $56,000. Most retirees can budget to allow themselves and their spouse (if married) to maintain their household expenses. However, long-term care often destroys a couple's budget because they are forced to maintain two households instead of just one.

Two types of insurance are available to cover expenses not paid by Medicare:

MEDICARE SUPPLEMENT INSURANCE
&
LONG-TERM CARE INSURANCE.

Medicare supplement or "Medigap" insurance is designed to cover Medicare insurance shortfalls for hospitalization, prescription drugs, and physician's fees. Since several types of Medigap coverage are available, be sure to study and understand the pros and cons of each before making a decision to purchase one.

Long-term care insurance coverage can pay for expenses incurred when care is provided at home or in an assisted living or nursing home facility. This topic is discussed more fully in the following chapter.

Frequently, I hear how expensive long-term care insurance is and what a waste of money it would be if you never use it. Let's review the reality of the odds of risk you face in life:

- The risk of using auto insurance is 1 in 240.
- The risk of having your home burn down is 1 in 1,200.
- The risk of needing long-term care or assisted living is 2 out of 5.

I have witnessed the financial devastation that unplanned health care expenses can cause. I'm not here to sell you on insurance, I'm suggesting you get a plan for your long-term medical expenses.

CHAPTER 22

Long-Term Care Insurance

Rule No. 1: Never lose money.
Rule No. 2: Never forget rule No. 1.

–WARREN BUFFETT–
INVESTMENT ENTREPRENEUR

Long-term care insurance helps pay the cost of assistance with the activities of daily living such as bathing and dressing. It also covers the kind of care you would need for a severe cognitive impairment like Alzheimer's. Depending upon the plan, it can also include skilled, intermediate and custodial care in your home, an adult day care center, an assisted living facility, a nursing home, or a hospice facility.

FORMER MILLIONAIRE STORY

Lesson: Paying for Long-Term Care

NAME: Jeff
AGE: 83
NET WORTH: Approx. $250,000
(previously $1.4 million)

Jeff is 83-years-old. His wife has been in a nursing home with Alzheimer's disease for over 15 years. When she was first diagnosed, Jeff and his wife had a net worth of approximately 1.4 million dollars. He had no long-term care insurance and because of his and his wife's net worth, he did not qualify for governmental assistance.

Like many who are married to Alzheimer's patients, Jeff now must bear the cost of maintaining two households. One for his wife in a nursing facility (with round the clock care) and the second for himself in his traditional family home.

The cost of care for Jeff's wife runs approximately $54,000 per year, which has forced Jeff to sell investment assets in order to pay for her care. So essentially, over the last 15 years Jeff and his wife have gone from being millionaires to being almost destitute. Unfortunately for Jeff, there is no way to recoup his losses because the principal has been consumed.

A lesson to be learned from Jeff's situation is that because of medical costs, even millionaires go broke and it is prudent to have a plan to address the staggering cost of long-term care.

Long term care is expensive and getting more expensive all the time. According to the MetLife Market Survey of Nursing Home and Home Care Costs, April 2002, the national average cost of a semi- private room in a nursing home is $52,000 annually. Home health care is expensive, too. The national average annual cost of home health care is well over $20,000 (that's $18/hour, five hours per day, five days a week for a home health aide).

Nursing home costs have been increasing about 5% a year. If this trend continues for another 30 years, the cost of nursing home care (for a semi-private room) in 2032 is expected to reach $190,600 a year. As you plan for the future, should consider whether this is an expense you will be able to afford.

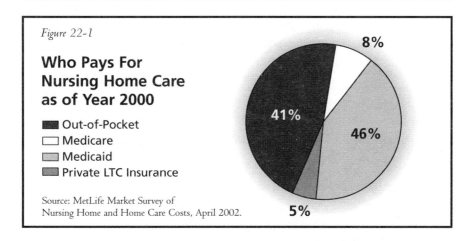

Figure 22-1

Who Pays For Nursing Home Care as of Year 2000

- ■ Out-of-Pocket
- ☐ Medicare
- ▨ Medicaid
- ▨ Private LTC Insurance

Source: MetLife Market Survey of Nursing Home and Home Care Costs, April 2002.

8%

41%

46%

5%

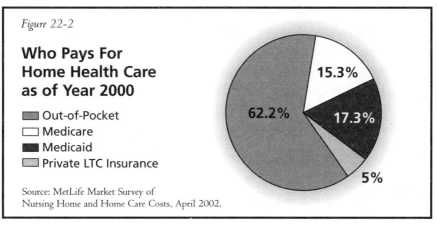

Figure 22-2

Who Pays For Home Health Care as of Year 2000

- ▨ Out-of-Pocket
- ☐ Medicare
- ■ Medicaid
- ▨ Private LTC Insurance

Source: MetLife Market Survey of Nursing Home and Home Care Costs, April 2002.

15.3%

62.2%

17.3%

5%

Some retirees think that long-term care is covered by their health plan or disability insurance, but that's usually not the case. Health insurance is designed to cover medical care for illnesses or injuries, such as cancer, a broken arm, or a stroke. Long-term care insurance is an excellent way to protect yourself from these expenses. You should consider buying long term care insurance if:

- You have assets and income you want to protect
- You want to avoid being financially dependent on others
- You want to maintain a choice of how and where to receive care

Long-term care insurance is not for everyone. If paying the premiums would adversely affect your standard of living or if you would quickly qualify for Medicaid, a long-term policy would not make sense. The process of investigating long-term care insurance begins with identifying potential insurance companies. After you narrow your search to a few companies or insurance agents, consider the following:

- Check with insurance rating services to make sure the insurance company you are considering is financially secure.
- Make sure the insurance agent is licensed to sell long term care insurance in your state.
- Review all the details and options of the policies. Do not rely solely on the marketing materials or outline of coverage.
- Make sure you understand all the provisions before you purchase any policy.
- Discuss policies with family members and others whose opinions you respect.
- Don't be pressured into making quick decisions.

Selecting the right long term care insurance policy will offer you and your family financial security, peace of mind and choice in care settings for the future.

Because long term care insurance premiums are based on age at the time of purchase, the younger you are when you purchase a policy, the less expensive it will be. Premiums for most policies stay level each year as you age (unless they are increased for all policyholders at once). If you buy at age 50, a typical policy may cost $800 per year. However, if you wait until age 65, the cost of that same policy could double.

BUYING LONG-TERM CARE INSURANCE

You can purchase long-term care insurance from a number of sources:

- Insurance agents and brokers, including companies that sell many other insurance

- Some financial planners
- Some continuing-care retirement communities
- Banks
- Employers who offer it as part of a benefits package
- Large membership organizations

More than 110 companies now offer long-term care insurance products, according to the Health Insurance Association of America. Contact your state Insurance Commissioner's office for a list of companies authorized to sell long-term care insurance in your state. Investigate the financial health of any insurance company that you are considering. Look for ratings from insurance rating services, such as A.M. Best, Moody's or Standard & Poor's. The insurance company should be rated in one of the top two categories by at least two services and have no low ratings. You can find these rating services in the reference section of your library.

Long-term care insurance may be sold directly to individuals or through an employer group or other organization. While groups do not usually offer a choice of companies, their advantage is that your organization has probably researched and selected a company and policy that will benefit its members. However, the policy offered may contain fewer choices in the amounts of coverage and options.

The most important factor in selecting a long-term care policy are the conditions required to qualify for coverage. Buying a policy to cover long-term care services will not help if you do not qualify for benefits. Many policies require a policyholder to have a cognitive or physical impairment for benefits to be paid.

I. Cognitive Impairment

People who are cognitively impaired typically have Alzheimer's disease or other forms of dementia. A policy's definition of cognitive impairment should not refer to the activities of daily living (ADL) since people with dementia usually can perform them.

2. Physical Impairment

People who have a physical impairment need assistance with the ADL, such as eating, dressing, transferring (e.g., out of bed to a chair), bathing and taking medications. Policies differ in the number of impairments a person must have before they qualify for benefits.

Another important factor is who decides whether or not you qualify for benefits. The decision maker is often called a "gatekeeper." Most policies require a licensed health care practitioner to write a plan of care. Some insurance companies offer a care (or case) manager to determine if you qualify or continue to qualify for benefits.

Long-term care expenses can be covered completely or in part by long-term care insurance. Policies pay a daily maximum amount for covered services. When you buy a policy, you decide the value of the daily maximum amount and the length of time your benefits will run. Most plans let you choose the amount of the coverage you want, as well as how and where you want to use your benefits. A comprehensive plan includes benefits for all levels of care, custodial to skilled. No policy guarantees to cover all costs of long-term care without limitation.

Many features can be included in long-term care insurance policies. Most companies offer you various choices including:

Benefit Amount

The daily maximum amount that a policy will pay for each days care. Usually, you can choose an amount between $50 and $400 per day.

Inflation Adjustment

It increases the benefit amount to cover the impact of inflation. Generally, companies offer a five percent inflation protection.

Benefit Period

The length of time the policy will pay for covered services. You can generally select a period of from 2 to 6 years or opt for a lifetime policy.

Deductible Period

The number of days required before the policy pays for care (also called "elimination period"). Elimination periods are typically 0 to 100 days.

Type of Care

Nursing home only, home care only or a whole continuum of care.

Non-forfeiture Benefits

If you stop paying premiums, you still receive some benefit from the policy. This protection will significantly raise your premiums.

WHAT DOES A GOOD LONG-TERM CARE POLICY COVER?

1. All levels of care in nursing facilities and other residential care settings, such as assisted living.
2. Under home care, the policy should include the community services of adult day care, respite care (temporary overnight care to relieve family caregivers) and hospice care. Policies should cover personal care.

Make sure that any policy you buy:

- Does not require prior hospitalization as a condition to receiving benefits.
- Is guaranteed renewable as long as you pay the premium. (This does not mean that premiums cannot be raised.)
- Offers a premium waiver while you are receiving benefits.
- Has one deductible for the life of the policy.

- Covers pre-existing conditions without a waiting period, provided pre-existing conditions were disclosed when you applied for the policy.
- Offers five percent (5%) compound inflation protection.
- Allows policyholders to upgrade or downgrade their coverage if they cannot afford premiums.

Assisted living residence services are either covered under home care or alternate care or may be a separate policy benefit. Some policies cover assisted living residences under nursing facility benefits. If you are interested in assisted living coverage, make sure you know how the policy handles this coverage.

Like all insurance, long-term care insurance policies contain limitations and exclusions. In general, long-term care may not be covered if it is required because of the following conditions:

- Alcohol and drug addiction;
- Illnesses caused by an act of war;
- Wounds resulting from intentionally self-inflicted injury, such as attempted suicide; and,
- Treatment already paid for by the government.

Long-term care insurance policy premiums are determined by:

- age;
- health;
- length of deductible;
- benefit amount paid; and,
- duration of benefits.

Higher daily benefits and optional features increase the premium. According to the Health Insurance Association of America, the annual premium for a low-option policy for a person age 50 is about $850; at 65 that same policy costs about $1,800; and at 79, about $5,500 per year.

Review the actual policy before buying it. Your agent should be willing to leave a sample policy for you to review. After you buy, you usually have the right to review the policy for 30 days with an option to cancel for a full refund.

Situations may also exist in rare cases where it makes sense to cancel an existing policy to buy a new one. Carefully compare the increased premiums with the added benefits of the new policy. Remember that your premium is based on your age at the time you initially purchase the policy. Insurance companies introduce new products every few years. Be sure to ask your agent about the company's practices regarding policy upgrades.

Since January 1, 1997, individuals have been able to include out-of-pocket expenses for long term-care and long-term care insurance premiums with their other itemized medical expenses on their annual federal income tax returns. Long-term care and other medical expenses are deductible, to the extent that they exceed the federal government's 7.5 percent threshold of adjusted gross income. The insurance benefits consumers receive, for the most part, will not be taxable as income.

Benefits paid under a long-term care insurance policy will not be treated as income for federal tax purposes. However, policies that pay a fixed sum per day in excess of $175 will be considered income. The $175 daily limit will rise with inflation in future years. A number of states have also recognized the importance of long-term care insurance by providing their own tax incentives.

Long term-care insurance can protect your assets and inheritance for your family, give you greater choice in selecting long-term care settings and provide you and your family with financial security. Remember to carefully consider how much insurance to buy and the options you need.

Finding a good policy will take some effort, but the result will be worthwhile.

- Talk to your financial planner or insurance agent about the advantages of long-term care insurance in your particular situation.

- Investigate sources on your own at various websites.
- Call your state government's Office on Aging or Insurance Department for information.

There is no one best policy. However, with some research and discussion with your financial advisor and family, you will find a policy that affordably fits your present lifestyle and future needs.

CHAPTER 23

Maids and Live-in Servants

When prosperity comes, do not use all of it.

– CONFUCIUS –

PHILOSOPHER

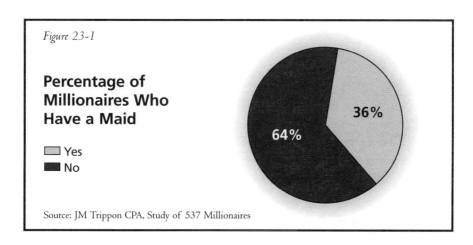

Figure 23-1

Percentage of Millionaires Who Have a Maid

- ▨ Yes
- ▧ No

36%

64%

Source: JM Trippon CPA, Study of 537 Millionaires

All of us know how hard it is to keep our homes clean and tidy. It is a never-ending chore that consumes much of our free time. In retirement, however, you may find that having help, such as a cleaning person or a live-in servant, is more significant than keeping your home clean. It may be a form of long-term care. Since people now live longer and often choose to stay in their own homes, outside help is often required. Help may come in the form of assistance with chores that you are no longer able to do or as we discussed in our last chapter, in the form of in-home health care.

Maybe you relish the thought of having a housekeeper or live-in help. Or maybe you've heard too many horror stories. Your sister-in-law hired a maid from an ad in the newspaper and came home to find her money gone. A friend told you about the housekeeper she hired who fell down the steps and your friend is still paying for the medical bills. Don't despair; basic knowledge about the potential problems of hiring a cleaning person or live-in will relieve your concerns. One of the most cost-effective and flexible arrangements for home care can be finding someone to live with you. While sharing your home with a home care worker takes some adjustment, it can provide some key advantages for those willing to try. You get a convenient, economical source of help at home and avoid or postpone being placed in a residential care facility. And the home care worker gets an important fringe benefit—a place to live.

The cost of live-in care is relatively economical, although rates vary significantly depending on the region where you live, hours needed and level of care. A free room will seldom mean an "even trade" for work. Nonetheless, providing room and board will considerably offset the overall cost of care. Check your newspaper housing section for the going rate for a room rental. Then, you can establish the wages you will have to pay based on a reasonable hourly rate or a monthly stipend. Some long- term-care insurance will cover patients who have a medical diagnosis that requires live-in help.

Two basic options are available when hiring a cleaning person or live-in. The first option is to hire a private individual, as has been the traditional source of domestic help for centuries! Hiring private help remains as popular an alternative as ever. The second option is to hire through a professional agency. An agency functions like a temporary employment agency and provides help on request.

Hiring private individuals has advantages and important complications. The most common advantage is cost. Usually, it is possible to hire private help for considerably less than through an agency. The money you save does not necessarily mean that you will be getting poorer quality. By choosing judiciously, you can find someone who is quality minded at an acceptable price.

Another advantage of employing a private individual is the added flexibility. Most agencies have restrictions against their people doing certain chores. A private party will usually perform those chores at no additional cost.

As appealing as another set of helping hands may sound, there are disadvantages to hiring private parties. The first is due to new tax laws and new interpretations of existing laws. Rather than being self-employed, maids or live-in housekeeper are generally considered to be your employees which opens an entire can of worms in the area of taxes.

Although these taxes are irritating, they pale in view of the liability you can incur when a private person cleans your house. If your house cleaner slips and falls while mopping the kitchen floor and breaks an ankle in the process, you could be held legally responsible for the injuries incurred. You could be sued for actual medical expenses and lost wages during the house cleaner's recovery! If the accident was due to negligence on your part, you could incur additional liability.

Another area of concern is lack of accountability. If your maid breaks something while cleaning, your only option is to try to charge the maid for it or try to file a claim under your homeowner's policy. Unfortunately, most policies do not cover such damage unless it's caused by vandalism. Likewise, forget about getting the maid to pay.

Theft is also a huge concern. Most homeowner's policies cover theft. However, before paying your claim, they require you to file a police report and pursue charges against the thief. In addition, these claims can also lead to higher premiums.

If these problems don't concern you, there are several places to hire a private maid. The most common is the help wanted section of your local newspaper. Another good source may be found in local churches. Many churches have some network of connecting people needing work with those wanting to hire. Don't ignore your local colleges either. Most have a job placement program that matches your needs with willing applicants. Naturally, the very best place to find a maid is from a friend or acquaintance currently using a maid who is seeking more work. No matter where you get potential help, always ask for several references and check them all!

HIRING FROM AGENCIES

With all the complications involved in hiring private house cleaners, the trend has recently been toward hiring through professional agencies. In recent years, maid services have been one of the fastest growing segments of the service industry.

The advantages of using an agency are many. Most agencies take on the responsibility of being the worker's employer. A reputable company works to protect you and your home. This is evident in their hiring practices.

Once you identify a prospective house cleaner , consider the following, most of which have to do with your safety and your peace of mind.

WHAT TO CHECK

1. **Bonding**

   Make sure the agency or individual is bonded. Should a theft occur, you should be protected.

2. **Insurance**

   Make sure the agency or individual is insured. If a maid or caregiver slips and falls, your homeowner's policy might not cover it.

3. **References**

   Make sure the agency or individual is reliable. Ask for written references and a detailed work history.

4. **Screening & Hiring**

   Check all references and the prospect's legal status to work in this country.

5. **Taxes**

   Make sure you don't break any tax laws. If housekeeper or maid earns at least $1300 per year, the law requires you to pay social security and other taxes for that person. Many agencies withhold taxes for their employees, but check to make sure.

6. **Worker's Compensation**

This is the insurance that covers the maid if he/she is hurt while cleaning your house. It will also protect you from having a claim filed against you.

LIVE-IN HELP

To prepare for interviewing prospective live-in helpers, make sure you have taken time to clearly define your needs. It is important to prescreen applicants by phone in order to get a sense of their experience and schedule. For example, could a student fulfill your work needs if he/she has classes during the day or in the evening? Be prepared to explain the basic duties the person will be expected to perform, your loved one's physical condition, and any special needs.

When hiring live-in help, chemistry is essential. You want someone whose personality meshes with yours. Remember, the person you hire will not become a family member, nor should he/she be treated as a guest. He/she will be an employee. For this reason, it is important to both of you to set boundaries. Consider the following:

- **Limit the hours.** Don't expect a live-in helper to work 24 hours a day. Provide a reasonable schedule with time off. If your situation requires your helper to be flexible, be sure to establish how he/she will be compensated for working extra hours or being "on call." In addition,

- **Respect Privacy**

  Give your helper adequate privacy during non-working hours in his/her bedroom and bathroom. Establish appropriate common areas of the house where he/she can relax.

- **Establish a Meal Schedule**

  Give your worker the option of eating his/her meals at established mealtimes or at other times, as long as his/her meals do not interrupt his/her duties.

- **Set a Phone Policy**

  Installing a second phone line for your live-in helper is a good idea and can eliminate problems regarding phone use and payment for long-distance calls. If you don't put in a separate phone, establish a clear phone policy.

- **Visiting Rules**

  Since your helper will be living in your home, it is reasonable for him/her to have guests. However, discuss and agree upon limits on visits such as number of visitors, reasonable times for visits, lengths of stay, use of the premises and long-term visitors.

TAXES ON DOMESTIC HELP

As if it isn't tough enough to find the right domestic help, you still have to worry about paying taxes as a household employer. So, rather than worry about it, prepare for it!

If you (1) hire someone to do house work, (2) control what work is done and (3) how that work is performed, you have engaged a household employee. It doesn't matter if you have hired him/her full or part time or how often you pay him/her.

Since you now have an employee, you must start thinking like an employer. First, obtain an Employer Identification Number (EIN) by obtaining and filing IRS form SS-4 or by calling the IRS.

It's against the law to employ an alien who isn't legally allowed to work in the United States. When you hire someone to work for you in your home, you and your employee are required to complete INS Form I-9, Employment Eligibility Verification. Your employee must complete the employee section of the form, and you, as employer, must then complete the employer section of Form I-9. Form I-9 requires you to examine documents presented by the employee to prove his/her identity and employment eligibility. Don't send Form I-9 to the government, but keep it with your records in a safe place—just in case you have to subsequently prove that your worker is not an illegal alien.

You're not required to withhold federal income taxes from the wages of household employees. We're not talking about withholding for Social Security and Medicare taxes here, only federal income tax withholding like that taken out of a corporate employee's paycheck. If your employee asks you to withhold federal (or state) income taxes, you may do so.

If you withhold federal income taxes, have your employee complete Form W-4. Note that if you and your employee choose not to withhold federal income taxes, it doesn't mean that the wages he/she receives are not subject to income tax! They are taxable and you're still required to issue a W-2 form to your employee.

Withholding for Social Security and Medicare taxes isn't optional. You are required by law to withhold and pay Social Security taxes, Medicare taxes, federal unemployment taxes and possibly state taxes on your household employee's wages if they exceed $1300 a year. As we go to press, Social Security and Medicare taxes amount to 15.3% of your employee's "gross" wages (basically, his/her hourly rate times the number of hours he/she works).

If you pay wages of $1,000 or more in any calendar quarter, then you must pay federal unemployment taxes for your household employees. Federal unemployment taxes are assessed on the first $7,000 of each employee's wages each year at the rate of 6.2% . However, you probably will have to pay state unemployment taxes as well. If so, you can take a credit of up to 5.4% against your federal unemployment tax liability to account for any state unemployment taxes you pay. This means that you typically pay only .8% in federal unemployment taxes on each employee's wages up to $7,000. Most states assesses unemployment taxes. Contact your state's unemployment tax agency for information regarding its wage base tax payment requirements.

So, after you have withheld taxes for your household employee, what do you do with the money? This is the easy part! Simply complete Schedule H of your federal tax return Form 1040 and attach it to your own income tax return when you file. If you feel that your tax obligations will be substantial, you may want to consider paying quarterly estimated tax payments.

Your household employee—like any other employee—must receive a W-2 form, which sets forth total wages you paid him/her that year. The W-2 form also lists the wages paid to the employee that were subject to Social Security and Medicare taxes along with the actual tax amounts. When you've completed Form W-2 for your employee, provide him or her with Copies B, C and 2 from the multi- part form. Then send Copy A to the Social Security Administration along with Form W-3. The instructions that accompany Form W-2 and Form W-3 explain the process.

Be sure to keep your records in a safe place. Retain your employment tax records for at least four years after you file your tax return with Schedule H.

For more information about household employee taxes, call the Internal Revenue Service at the number listed in your local telephone directory.

CHAPTER 24

Avoiding Investment Scams

You can't cheat an honest man.

– W.C. FIELDS –

COMEDIAN

Anyone can be a victim of fraud. Con artists however, often prey on wealthy retirees simply because of their wealth. Financial fraud, all too often, is absolutely devastating on a retiree's financial security. To maintain wealth during retirement, you must be savvy enough to spot and avoid fraudulent schemes.

The following millionaire story shows how important it is to check out the people you invest with.

MILLIONAIRE STORY

Lesson: Check Out Who You Do Business With

NAME:	Charles
AGE:	55
NET WORTH:	$1.9 million

Charles, a 55-year-old corporate executive had always been conservative with his own personal investments and yet he almost fell victim to a common investment scam.

Charles was introduced to an "investment advisor" by a friend from work. The investment advisor told Charles that he could receive a tremendously high rate of return by investing in venture capital deals. Charles called me and asked me to liquidate some of the conservative

---

investments in his portfolio in order to raise cash to buy into one of these "opportunities."

Prior to transferring the funds to this new advisor, Charles asked me to do a quick background check. I contacted the National Association of Securities Dealers and was amazed by what I found. The supposed "investment advisor" did not have a securities license and was not even affiliated with the brokerage firm he said he was. It also turned out that he had defrauded dozens of people of their life savings.

Fortunately for my client, we were able to discover that the "investment advisor" was a crook before Charles gave him any of his funds. Unfortunately, Charles's friends were not all so lucky. Total losses by Charles's friends ran into millions. The lesson to be learned from this story is always checkout the people you plan to invest with before you make the investment.

In this chapter we will explore some of the more common investment scams and some ideas to avoid them. A recent government report issued by state securities regulators listed the following as the "Top 10 Investment Scams."

"Top 10 Investment Scams" courtesy of the North American Securities Administrators Association, ranked roughly in order of prevalence or concern:

I. **Unlicensed Individuals,**

such as life insurance agents, selling securities. To verify that an individual is licensed or registered to sell securities, call your state securities regulator. If the person is not registered, don't invest. In Indiana, 11 of the 16 "cease and desist" orders issued by the Securities Division in the first quarter of 2003 targeted insurance agents who sold securities without the proper license. Most of them were independent life insurance agents.

2. Affinity Group Fraud

Many scammers use their victim's religious or ethnic identity to gain their trust. They capitalize on the fact that it's human nature to trust people who are like you—and once they gain your trust, they won't hesitate to try to steal your life savings. No group is safe from con artists who seek to exploit others in the group for their personal financial gain. They hit church "gifting" programs and minorities who fall for foreign exchange scams. In Texas, an Indian immigrant who taught Sunday school took fellow Indian parishioners—roughly 40 families in all—for over $1 million.

3. Payphone & ATM Sales

In early 2003, 25 states and the District of Columbia announced actions against companies and individuals—many of them independent life insurance agents—that took roughly 4,500 people for $76 million by selling coin-operated customer-owned telephones. Investors leased payphones for between $5,000 and $7,000 and were promised annual returns of up to 15 percent. Regulators say the largest of these investments appeared to be nothing but Ponzi schemes (See item no. 6 below).

4. Promissory Notes

Short-term debt instruments issued by little-known or sometimes non-existent companies that promise high returns—upwards of 15 percent monthly—with little or no risk. These notes are often sold to investors by independent life insurance agents. In Indiana, 18 elderly investors lost some $1.4 million in a promissory note scam. An 80-year-old woman lost her life savings of $324,000. The perpetrators—who diverted the money to offshore bank accounts, made first-class business trips to China, India and Greece and bought expensive cars. They even knelt in prayer with their victims to gain their trust.

5. Internet Fraud

Scammers use the wide reach and supposed anonymity of the Internet to "pump and dump" thinly traded stocks, peddle bogus offshore "prime bank" investments and publicize pyramid schemes. Roughly half the states now have Internet surveillance programs that watch for fraud or investigate investor complaints. Regulators urge investors to ignore anonymous financial advice on the Internet and in chat rooms.

6. **Ponzi/Pyramid Schemes**

These swindles promise high returns to investors, but the only ones who consistently make money are the promoters who set these scams in motion. Ponzi and pyramid schemes use money from previous investors to pay new investors. They build a house of cards that inevitably collapse. Ponzi schemes are the legacy of Italian immigrant Charles Ponzi, who in the early 1900s, took investors for $10 million by promising 40 percent returns from arbitrage profits on International Postal Reply Coupons.

7. **"Callable" CDs**

High-yielding certificates of deposit that won't mature for 10- to 20-years unless the bank, not the investor, "calls," or redeems, them. Redeeming a CD early may result in large losses—upwards of 25 percent of the original investment. In Iowa, for example, a retiree in her 70s invested over $100,000 of her 97-year-old mother's money in three "callable" CDs with 20-year maturities. Her intention, she told her broker, was to use the money to pay her mother's nursing home bills. Regulators say sellers of callable CDs often don't adequately disclose the risks and restrictions.

8. **Viatical Settlements**

Originated to help the gravely ill pay their bills, these interests in the death benefits of terminally ill patients are always risky and sometimes fraudulent. The insured gets a percentage of the death benefit in his/her life insurance policy in cash and investors, in exchange, receive the death benefit when the insured dies. Because of the uncertainty of predicting when someone will die, these investments are extremely speculative. In a new twist, Pennsylvania regulators say "senior settlements"—interests in the death benefits of healthy older people—are now being offered to investors.

Chapter Twenty-Four

9. **Prime Bank Schemes**

Scammers promise investors triple-digit returns through access to the investment portfolios of the world's elite banks. Purveyors of these schemes often target conspiracy theorists, promising access to the "secret" investments used by the Rothschild's or Saudi royalty. In North Dakota, state securities regulators have alleged that a small group of salesmen, including a local pastor, used religious and family ties to bilk investors out of $2 million in a prime bank scam.

10. **Investment Seminars**

Often the only people getting rich are those hosting the seminars, which make money from high admission fees and the sale of books, audiotapes and their services. These seminars are marketed through newspaper, radio and TV ads and "infomercials." Regulators urge investors to be extremely skeptical about any get-rich-quick scheme.

W.C. Fields once said: "You can't cheat an honest man". And the key to protecting yourself is not to be lured by greed into a scam run by a shady operator.

Con men (and women) count on you overlooking your normal investment standards in trying to entice you into one of these deals.

AVOIDING RIP OFFS

What steps should you take to avoid being ripped off? I recommend the following 10-point system for staying out of trouble:

1. **Trust your gut instincts.** If an investment sounds too good to be true it probably is and you should politely decline to pursue it.

2. **Run it by advisors you trust.** Before making an investment, run it by your trusted advisors such as your "Comprehensive Financial Advisor", your CPA, your attorney, and of course, your spouse.

3. **Only invest with reputable firms such as members of the NASD, NYSE and SIPC.** If buying securities, only do business with investment companies, which are members of the NASD (National Association of Securities Dealers) or NYSE (New York Stock

Exchange) and the SIPC (Securities Investors Protection Corporation.)

4. **If a security is not publicly traded, don't buy it.** Never buy a security that is not already publicly traded with a verifiable history. Never buy a "private placement," "limited partnership," "precious metal," "viatical settlement," or "promissory note investment."

5. **Never buy any investment over the phone from someone you don't know.**

6. **Get the brokers license number and check their background.** Ask if the investment broker who you are speaking with is licensed with the NASD and obtain their CRD# (their federal registration number) and then check their background by contacting the NASD public disclosure program on the internet at www.nasdr.com. You will be able to learn how long the broker has been in business and what complaints (if any) are on their record.

7. **If buying insurance, verify it is licensed for sale in your state.** If you are buying an insurance product verify both the product and the broker selling it are licensed with your state department of insurance or insurance commissioner. You can generally reach this department by contacting directory assistance in your state capital. Or you can locate your state insurance commissioner information from the National Association of Insurance Commissioners on the Internet www.naic.org.

8. **Check the financial ratings.** If you are buying an insurance product also verify the insurance carrier's financial strength rating from the major rating agencies:

A.M. Best
Duff & Phelps
Standard & Poors.

9. **Use restrictive endorsements.** When buying an investment always make your check payable to the investment company using a restrictive endorsement. If you are opening an account with ABC brokerage and your name is John Smith, write your check as follows:

"ABC Brokerage FBO John Smith"

The letters FBO stand for "For the Benefit Of" which means that it can only be deposited into your account at ABC Brokerage. Never make your investment check payable to the individual selling the investment and never pay cash when you invest. Reputable investment companies will not accept cash investments.

10. **Get it in writing.** Get a copy of everything you sign and all account-opening documents, prospectuses and product disclosures.

The bottom line when it comes to scams is using common sense. Don't let greed trick you into foolish investments. Do your homework by investigating before you buy anything!

CHAPTER 25

Second Marriages & Money

When love comes in the front door...
common sense goes out the window.
– ROMANIAN PROVERB –

Remember that list of common unexpected catastrophic expenses in Chapter 20? The most devasting financial surprise (after healthcare and investment scams) is debts acquired in remarriage.

MILLIONAIRE STORY

Lesson: Be Careful Whom You Marry

NAME:	Laura
AGE:	35
NET WORTH:	$1.1 million

Laura, a beautiful 35-year-old single parent, inherited $750,000 from her grandmother. Her husband (now ex-husband) tried to steal the funds, which fortunately for Laura were tied up in a trust. Because of the way her assets were structured, Laura's philandering ex-husband was not able to abscond from any of Laura's money.

The lesson to be learned is to checkout the personal and financial history of any perspective spouse before saying "I do." They say that love is blind, however, there is a price to be paid for blindness, particularly to your net worth when you marry the wrong person. Do your homework!

According to a recent study, over 40% of all marriages are remarriages. Most of us have heard the statistic that roughly half of all marriages end in divorce.

Many retirees remarry after being widowed. Regardless of the reason, professional counselor's report that finances are the root cause of most marital problems . This chapter covers common financial issues for retirees who are about to enter into a second marriage.

FINANCIAL DISCUSSIONS

Marriage is a time for a new beginning. Love and hope create an opportunity for a new life together. Marriage can also create a financial nightmare for both parties involved and their children.

Before any of my clients get married, I always encourage the couple to come in for financial counseling. I find that the prospective bride and groom frequently have discussed everything, except money.

A great starting point is to look at each person's assets and debts. Then review each of their credit reports and financial statements. This provides insight into how each handles financial responsibility and facilitates a discussion of their spending plans, savings, budgets, and investments.

I encourage you have such a financial discussion moderated by an independent third party since it can be an emotional session.

Financial Issues to Discuss before Marriage

1. Assets, including savings, investments, real estate and retirement accounts
2. Existing debts including mortgages, auto loans, & most importantly, credit cards
3. Obligations under a previous divorce decree
4. Unpaid taxes whether Federal or State
5. Credit reports & credit ratings
6. Expected joint income & cost of living
7. Pre-nuptial agreements or premarital trusts
8. Inheritances & beneficiary arrangements for children.

9. Wills

10. Insurance

Let's examine some of these topics in more detail.

Assets

You each must make a list of all of your assets in order to assess your new "joint" financial position. Also, discuss the amount of money you would like to save to feel comfortable. Discuss your investment goals and philosophies. Determine where you will live and if you both own houses, whether one property will be sold, and if so, whose and how the proceeds will be disbursed.

Debts

Both parties must reveal all existing debt including mortgages, auto loans, unpaid taxes and most importantly, credit card debt. Unless all debt is disclosed, an innocent spouse could inherit financial responsibility for the new spouse's prior debts.

Obligations under a Previous Divorce Decree

Marital obligations are similar debts except that the legal system is often involved in setting payments. I know of several cases where a retired wife had to return to work to help pay her new husband's child support or alimony obligations. Worse yet are cases in which the new wife's assets were seized to pay the new husband's delinquent child support payments, because they had commingled their accounts.

Unpaid Federal or State Taxes

Although the IRS has programs that ostensibly exist to protect innocent spouse from their new partner's prior debts, in reality, the IRS wants to collect unpaid taxes and often will collect from the new, non-debtor spouse. To do so, it seizes joint bank accounts, joint investments, and your anticipated income tax refunds.

Credit Reports and Credit Ratings

This one is a must! Obtain and review a copy of each other's credit reports through one of the major reporting agencies such as Equifax or Experian. Credit reports can be most revealing. Business people won't take on new partners without checking their credit reports and neither should you!

Expected Joint Income and Cost of Living

Discuss your income, the categories of your living expenses, and how much you plan to spend on each. If one of you has little or no income, how will the bill payments be shared? If you both have income, write an agreement governing who will pay for what. Also, do you plan to keep separate bank accounts, have joint accounts or a combination of the two?

Pre-nuptial Agreements or Premarital Trusts

If either of you has substantial assets, income, or debts, discuss whether you should execute a pre- nuptial agreement or premarital trust. These documents are often advisable for three major reasons:

1. To keep certain property separate in the event of a future divorce;
2. To avoid having specific property seized for prior debts of a new spouse;
3. To prevent the disinheritance of children from a prior marriage.

Should you decide to use a "pre-nup", be aware that most states require that both parties be represented by legal counsel. Further, each party must hire and pay their own attorney. Even with these precautions, pre-nuptial agreements are often ruled invalid. Pre-nups are typically a difficult topic for couples to discuss, but they are important. Your best resource is an attorney with expertise in drafting and advising clients on pre-nuptial agreements.

A common alternative to a "pre-nup" agreement is a separate property trust. Under such a trust, the assets you plan to keep separate for the benefit of someone other than your new spouse (your children, for example) are placed in a trust. The trust protects the assets for the beneficiaries by preventing others, including new spouses, from gaining access to them. Get legal advice before attempting to set up a separate property trust.

One last point. If you plan to live together prior to marriage, be sure to learn the laws in your state regarding "common-law" marriage.

Wills

Remarriage is the time to update old wills because they typically designate your former spouse as a beneficiary. Also, upon remarriage, update any of your powers of attorney or medical directives (living wills, do not resuscitate orders or durable powers of attorney for healthcare). Think carefully about who you should name as your executor and how to balance the interests of children from your former marriage with the interests of your new spouse. Since friction between a person's children and his/her new spouse is common, name a strong, fair executor and leave clear instructions. Unclear instructions or a weak executor could cause an expensive challenge to your will.

Inheritances & Beneficiary Arrangements for Children

Typically, a new spouse will have a claim on your estate when you die. This means that you could inadvertently disinherit your children from an earlier marriage if you are not proactive. Normally, your new spouse will have to specifically waive his/her claim to all or a portion of your assets or those assets will not pass to your children. Arrangements that are fair to everyone can be structured, but you need to first discuss solutions to the problem and then get them implemented. For your protection, consult with and, have documents detailing your arrangement written by, an attorney.

Insurance

Remarriage is also an idea time to review your insurance needs as well as change beneficiaries on existing insurance policies.

CHAPTER 26

Fees and Commissions
A New Money Management Paradigm

Money can't buy poverty.
— MARTY FELDMAN —
COMEDIAN

In the investment management business, one topic guaranteed to create a spirited discussion is fees and commissions. Although fees and commissions are not on the list of money consuming catastrophes, they certainly qualify as a "money gobbler." Many different approaches exist for fees and commissions.

On one extreme are some of the traditional investment brokerage firms. Their advertising seems to indicate that every investor should utilize full-commission brokerage firms for all transactions. These investment houses claim that investing is so complicated, it is impossible to manage on your own and that the value your advisor adds is worth any price he cares to charge. Often, these charges run 2 to 4 percent of the total account value each year.

On the other extreme are the "do it yourself" financial magazines and no-load mutual fund firms. Their advertising implies that investment management is so easy that only a fool would pay a fee or commission to manage his/her account. During the heyday of the 1999 dot-com stock frenzy, some of the advertising for online brokerage firms was absolutely outrageous. I remember television ads that encouraged investors to quit their jobs for the thrills and riches to be found in day trading. Yeah right, quit your job to become a professional gambler, and use your life savings to make the bets.

As an advisor, I've seen problems with both of the models described above.

On one hand, I have met prospective clients who paid full-service brokers a yearly 3% "management fee" to oversee cash accounts that were invested in money market funds that earned approximately 1.6%. As both a CPA and an investment advisor, I fail to see the logic in recommending a financial transaction whose best-case scenario results in a loss to the client.

On the other hand, I also met a 62-year-old business owner who self managed his accounts and "saved commissions" by trading online. The results—He turned a $700,000 portfolio into less than $9,000. Hey, but at least he didn't pay commissions.

Let's review the traditional options most investors have in managing their money:

1. Hire a traditional "stock broker," bank or institution to actively make all money management decisions and pay them handsome fees for the privilege or

2. Self manage your funds. Self management would include doing : all of your own research, trading, or perhaps, even buying your stocks commission free via a dividend reinvestment plan. Or, in the alternative, selecting no-load mutual funds through either television ads or "do-it-yourself financial magazines."

Often in life, the ideal answer to a dilemma involving two extremes lies somewhere in the middle. I believe that the ideal solution is what I refer to as the "new money management paradigm."

THE NEW MONEY MANAGEMENT PARADIGM ASSUMES

- You need an advisor. Both investment management and tax planning are complicated and rapidly changing areas. They require more time and expertise than most retirees are able or willing to spend. What you don't know can hurt you.

- You and your advisor should work together as a team. He/she should not make the money management decisions alone and you should carefully and objectively consider his/her advice.

- Your advisor should be well paid. Top professionals are worth what they charge and often will make you money. However, ask a potential advisor exactly what you are paying him/her for and reserve the right to terminate the relationship at any time.

- Your advisor should never take custody of your money, receive checks in his/her name or have check- writing authority for your accounts. Reputable investment companies prohibit this type of practice. Instead, maintain control of all your funds by placing them directly in your own accounts at financial institutions.

ADVISOR COSTS

What will an independent financial advisor cost you? Typically they charge a fee based on the amount of funds they manage in your account. For example, they may charge 1.25% to 1.5% per year of the invested value of your account plus transaction fees . If you agree to pay advisory fees, always get a fee disclosure form called an ADV form Part II before you invest any funds.

If your advisor works on a commission basis, rather than a fee basis, obtain a copy of their commission schedule as well as a prospectus before investing. Commission amounts should not exceed what you would have paid on a fee basis over the estimated duration of the investment.

Perhaps an example will help you. Let's assume you are considering two different investment advisors. The first advisor does not charge commissions but does charge an asset management fee of 1.5% per year of all amounts he manages for you.

The second advisor does not charge asset management fees but is recommending a mutual fund that bears an up-front load (commission) of 5.75%.

In this case it would take almost four years for the fees charged by the first advisor to catch up with the commission costs from the second advisor.

Also, we have to ask the question, if the second advisor is not being paid a management fee, what type of service will we be getting in future years when changes in the economy or our circumstances would dictate the need for changes in our portfolio?

The issue of service is one reason many clients now choose a fee based approach.

Also bear in mind that most independent advisors have a minimum-account-size requirement. Few independent advisors accept accounts of less than $50,000. Many will only work with account minimums of $250,000, $500,000 or $1 million.

For more assistance in selecting the right financial advisor for you, see Chapter 16, which explores this topic in greater detail.

CHAPTER 27

Life Insurance in Retirement

Being rich is having money;
being wealthy is having time.
— MARGARET BONNANO —
WRITER

Earlier in the book, I suggested that you should not purchase more insurance than you need. When I talk about life insurance I surprise a lot of my clients because they assume that I am going to try and sell them more life insurance. Often the opposite is true: I advise my retiree clients to cancel insurance policies they no longer need. I believe that it is my duty to save my clients' money and help to ensure them a retirement where they can "Stay Rich Forever."

Life insurance needs vary at different stages of our lives. When we are just starting our careers, it makes sense to buy life insurance to fund shortfalls that would occur if we died prematurely.

For example, if a 25-year-old man with two infant children is killed in an automobile accident, his family would definitely benefit from the fact that he had life insurance. Since he died at 25, he would not have had the opportunity to work long enough to pay off the family mortgage, save for his children's' college, or fund his retirement plan. Insurance could cover these shortfalls.

On the other hand, if the same man died at age 65, he probably would have already funded his childrens' college, paid off the mortgage, and provided adequate savings for retirement. At this point, would he still need life insurance (or at least as much)? Often, the answer is no, because he might already have liquidated the need for life insurance by paying off his debts and building a solid asset base.

What are the legitimate reasons to maintain life insurance during retirement? The most common are:

1. to pay income or estate taxes triggered by death;
2. to replace or maximize income from a single life company pension;
3. to ensure that children from a previous marriage receive their fair inheritance;
4. to fund a child's trust;
5 to fund a charitable legacy.

The following millionaire story illustrates this point.

MILLIONAIRE STORY

Lesson: Life Insurance and Insurance

NAME:	Frank
AGE:	68
NET WORTH:	$4.0 million

Frank, a 68-year-old retired engineer, maintained most of his net worth in his retirement accounts. Upon his death, when his estate is distributed to his heirs, the tax liability these funds would exceed $2.0 million.

In Frank's case, we determined it was less expensive to purchase insurance to fund the taxes than to pay the taxes from the funds in his estate. Since Frank knew where he wanted his funds to go when he died, he wanted to make sure that he his estate would have sufficient funds. Therefore, he purchased insurance in an amount that would pay any tax liabilities.

The lesson to be learned is that after retirement, insurance may still be an important part of your portfolio.

TYPES OF INSURANCE

Most people who own life insurance really don't understand much about the policies they own. So, lets review the most common types of life insurance. They are:

Term Insurance

Provides a preset amount of cash if you die during the time period when the policy is in force. For example, a ten-year $1,000,000 term insurance policy will pay the face amount if you die within ten years and that's it. If you live beyond the ten-year term say to the twelfth year, you get nothing. With term insurance, you pay only for life insurance coverage. The policy does not develop cash value reserves.

Term insurance is the cheapest form of coverage over a limited number of years. Many types of term insurance are available, but all of them pay off only if you die during the policy time period. They pay nothing (zero) if you live beyond the policy period.

Term life insurance is usually good for young people with families who want substantial insurance coverage at reasonable rates. Since the risk of dying in your 20s, 30s or 40s is quite low, the cost of term insurance during these years is economical; life insurance prices don't get cheaper.

Term is your best choice if you need insurance for a short time, say to qualify for a business loan. However, the older you are, the more expensive term insurance premiums become. A 40 year old will pay more than a 20 year old on a policy with the same face value, which is understandable because the older you are, the greater the chance you will die during the policy term. If you want insurance coverage that will continue in force your entire life, term insurance isn't for you.

Whole Life

Provides a set dollar amount of coverage that cannot be canceled if fixed, uniform premium payments are paid. Since the premiums remain the same throughout your life, they are high in comparison to your statistical risk of death in the early policy years. Charging relatively high initial premiums is how reserves are built. If you live long after the policy was issued, your premiums, which have remained unchanged, will be low compared to your risk of death.

In other words, during the first few years of a whole life policy, insurance companies take in substantially more money than they pay out. These companies invest the surplus amounts they receive. Some of the surplus becomes your cash reserve, which grows over time. The cash reserve earns dividends, paid by the insurance company. After a set period of time, you have the right to borrow against the cash reserves in your policy. You can also, of course, cancel the policy and receive its cash surrender value.

Whole life insurance coverage often is not desirable for younger families who are not able to afford the high premium payments during the early policy years.

Universal Life Insurance

Universal life combines some desirable features of both term and whole life insurance but also carries more risk to the policyholder. Over time, the net cost of universal insurance usually runs lower than whole life insurance. However, changes in interest rates can cause your cost of insurance to soar. With universal life, you build up a cash reserve as with whole life. But you can also vary the premium payment amount, the amount of coverage, or both, from year to year. In contrast, whole life requires you to pay one set amount, which cannot be varied, for the life of the policy.

Universal life policies normally provide you with more consumer information than other policies. For example, they inform you how much of your premium goes toward company overhead expenses, reserves and policy proceed payments, and how much is retained for your savings. This information is not usually provided with whole life policies. Other significant features of universal life can be explained to you by an insurance agent.

Chapter Twenty-Seven

Second to Die / Survivorship Life

Second to Die insurance (also called "second to die" or "joint" insurance) is a relatively new type of insurance. It is a single policy that insures two lives, usually spouses. When the first spouse dies, no proceeds are paid. Instead, the policy remains in force and the surviving spouse must continue to pay premiums. The policy pays off only upon the death of the second spouse.

Why would a couple want such a policy? Mainly it could be advantageous to wealthier couples as part of an estate plan when they expect substantial estate taxes will be assessed on the death of the second spouse. Second to die and survivorship life policies are not advantageous to people with small or moderate-sized estates.

Second to die or survivorship life insurance may also be desirable when the survivors do not wish to sell a major asset that is not liquid, like a valuable family business or real estate interests . For example, two children inherit a family business, but one doesn't want to keep it going. The other child could use his/her share of the insurance proceeds as an initial buy-out payment so that he/she could purchase ownership of the business.

Finally, second to die or survivorship life insurance may be beneficial if one member of a couple is in poor health and the purchase of other insurance would be extremely expensive. Since two lives are insured, premiums for survivorship life policies would be comparatively low compared to policies on one life. Therefore, if the other spouse is in reasonably good health, the couple can usually obtain survivorship life insurance.

GENERAL RULES FOR LIFE INSURANCE AT DIFFERENT STATIONS OF LIFE

I have some general rules for life insurance. However, always remember that your own personal situation is unique and that your insurance decisions should be made according to your personal facts and with a licensed insurance professional.

1. If your age is 20-49, term insurance will generally be your best insurance value. Insure a value equal to 15 times your income less any investment savings.

2. If you are in your 50s or older, or plan to hold the coverage until you die, you should carefully consider insurance types other than term.

3. Never allow premiums to be so high that they destroy your budget and radically reduce a normal lifestyle.

4. Don't expose yourself to loss of coverage from unrealistic coverage which is either too high or too low.

5. Shop price and rating together.

TAX
EFFICIENCY

CHAPTER 28

Phantom Income Tax

The hardest thing in the world to
understand is the income tax.
— ALBERT EINSTEIN —
PHYSICIST

The third pillar in building a sound financial house is to receive income in tax efficient ways. This section is devoted entirely to this pillar.

Millionaires are very clear about the need to manage their tax liabilities.

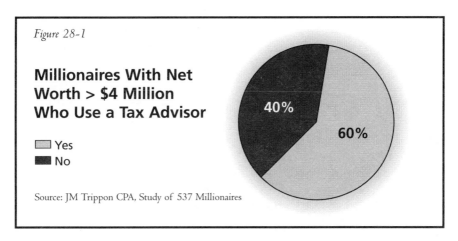

Figure 28-1

Millionaires With Net Worth > $4 Million Who Use a Tax Advisor

☐ Yes
■ No

40%

60%

Source: JM Trippon CPA, Study of 537 Millionaires

PHANTOM INCOME

To be tax efficient, we need to watch out for "phantom income." What in the world is phantom income? It sounds like something from a grade B movie, but in reality it is much scarier. CPAs define phantom income as reportable or taxable income that **does not generate any apparent cash flow.** Now that is scary!

For example, mutual funds continually move money in and out of stocks. If a stock is bought and sold within twelve (12) months, its profits and losses are taxed as ordinary income or losses, not as long term capital gains. At the end of the year, a fund may show a loss in market value, but if it realized "profits" from selling shares or receiving dividends during the year. In this case you will get a 1099 form showing that you had ordinary income, capital gains, and/or dividends. The income that the fund generated was only "phantom" income because although income was earned, many investors choose to reinvest it back into additional shares. If the market value of the shares account falls rapidly, you may find yourself paying tax on an account that is worth less at the end of the year than at its beginning.

> **In other words the account may fall in value to a greater extent than ordinary income, dividends and capital gains were generated. Hence you feel you have only received "phantom income." Nevertheless, you're required to pay taxes on your share of this "phantom income."**

A man attended one of my retirement planning workshops who had put $100,000 in Fidelity's Aggressive Growth fund in year 2000 because he read in an article that it was a great fund. By the end of the year the fund had lost 27 percent, so his money was down to $73,000. Do you think he got a tax deduction? No, because $12,000 in taxable "phantom" income was distributed on a 27 percent market value loss. He had to pay over $5,000 in income tax on an account that lost 27 percent. And what happened in year 2001? He lost another 47 percent and had to pay tax again for 2001 because income was distributed. His $100,000 went down to below $39,000 and he had to pay over $5,000 in income tax. Does that make sense to you? It doesn't make any sense to me, but that's the way mutual funds are often taxed. **Keep in mind that this is true only for investments held outside a retirement account and that have phantom income.**

MILLIONAIRE STORY

Lesson: Manage Your Phantom Income

NAME: Harry

AGE: 72

NET WORTH: $1.1 million

Harry, a 72-year-old retired business owner, had always reinvested his profits back into his business. Therefore, at time of retirement, he did not have substantial pension accounts, but instead had invested his money into taxable mutual funds.

The taxable mutual funds generated annual dividends and produced capital gains from trades made by the mutual fund managers. The dividends and capital gains obligated Harry and his wife to pay over $20,000.00 a year in income taxes on phantom income.

By restructuring Harry's investments into tax deferred accounts Harry was able to reduce his tax bill substantially, and not change his standard of living. The bottom line is that if you are receiving phantom income, you need to consider a restructuring of your holdings to make your investments more tax efficient.

Limited partnerships and family owned S corporations may also show profits, but not pay out any cash to their shareholders. The shareholder's percentage of profit is considered income for federal income tax purposes even though the taxpayer got no actual cash.

PREVENTING LOSSES

The good news is that many negative income tax consequences can be prevented. Rather than putting your money in taxable mutual funds, consider moving them to tax deferred holdings and avoid the tax burden.

I have a client named Pat. She owns her own home and has three (3) sources of income: a pension that brings in $25,000 a year;

Social Security of $15,000, and a $200,000 CD that yields 4 percent.

The CD was earning $8,000 a year, which Pat did not use for living expenses. She lived on her pension and social security moneys. Pat was required to pay tax of 66 percent of her Social Security benefits because of the money she earned from the CD and her pension. As a result, she paid $6,975 in taxes as a single individual at age 70.

Pat came to me and I suggested that we find a way to pay the government less and earn more interest. We took the money out of the CD and invested it in a fixed rate annuity at 6 percent interest. Pat's annuity is not subject to tax until she withdraws the money from this tax deferred vehicle.

The result is that Pat's tax bracket was lowered and she paid tax on only 25 percent of her social security benefit. Why? Because the interest income accruing inside the annuity is not taxable until it is withdrawn. The net result was a saving of $3,900 in taxes. Plus, Pat's income from the annuity actually was higher than it was in a CD!!

Tax deferred investing offers tremendous advantages. However, make sure you ask lots of questions, learn the penalties for early withdrawal, verify all fees and expenses, and understand what you are getting into before you invest!

Also, bear in mind that while the CD Pat purchased from the bank was covered by FDIC insurance in case of the bank's failure, the annuity was not protected by FDIC insurance and was instead subject to the financial strength of the annuity issuer. Accordingly, there is a risk of loss with annuities.

CHAPTER 29

Retirement Account Withdrawals
Tax Strategies

Income tax time is when
you test your powers of deduction.
— SHELBY FRIEDMAN —
WRITER

Tax strategies must be considered in every financial decision you make. As we previously discussed, if you have a company pension plan, you will usually be asked to choose a lump sum or a lifetime pension annuity at the time of your retirement. In general, I recommend the lump-sum option. (See Chapters 17 & 18)

If you choose the lump-sum option, however, be aware of the tax consequences. The taxable portion of a lump-sum distribution is the excess of the distribution over any nondeductible contributions made to the plan by the employee. This amount generally is ordinary income in the year of receipt to the extent it is not rolled over into an eligible retirement plan.

When a retiree receives funds in a lump-sum, he/she has three main options:

1. taking the distribution as a lump-sum in cash;

2. rolling the distribution over into a traditional IRA or rolling the distribution into a conduit IRA and converting it to a Roth IRA; and,

3. using 10-year tax averaging.

LUMP-SUM

If you take a lump-sum payment in cash, you will immediately lose a portion of it to taxes. What's more, you lose the benefit of tax deferral unless you reinvest the money in a tax-favored investment. Under tax deferral arrangements, future earnings will be taxed as they are earned. If you receive a $100,000 lump sum payment, you will immediately lose a mandatory 20% withholding tax, which will bring your actual payout to $80,000. Assuming that you are in a 30% tax bracket, you would incur an additional $10,000 in ordinary income tax. Thus, your original lump sum of $100,000 would actually end up being a lump sum payment of $70,000.

ROLLOVER

Another option is to deposit the money into a traditional IRA or other qualified retirement plan. Your money will grow tax-deferred until you withdraw it and then it will be taxed as ordinary income. Several different options exist for depositing a lump sum amount into an IRA or other qualified plan:

Arrange a direct rollover.

Have your current employer deposits your funds directly into a traditional IRA or other retirement plan. Since you never personally take receipt of your money, the IRS will not require your employer withhold 20% of the distribution. The entire distribution is rolled over into your new account.

Take receipt of the lump sum distribution and deposit it within 60 days into a traditional IRA or new retirement plan.

There are two big drawbacks to this option. (1) If you miss the 60-day deadline, even by a day, you will owe taxes on the entire sum. (2) If you take receipt of the money yourself, even for a short time, your employer must deduct 20% withholding tax from the total and you will receive only 80% of your money. The IRS will allow you to reinvest the gross distribution within 60 days, but, you will have to go into other funds to make up the 20% that has been withheld by the employer.

Convert your traditional IRA to a Roth IRA.

After your employer deposits your funds directly into a traditional IRA, you have the option to convert it to a Roth IRA. The Roth IRA allows you to withdraw earnings federal tax free, provided certain requirements are met. However, converting a traditional IRA to a Roth IRA would subject the entire balance in your traditional IRA, excluding non-deductible contributions, to income taxation. The decision to convert or retain an existing IRA usually involves some tradeoffs, so weigh your options carefully. Consult your financial professional or tax advisor to help you choose the best IRA option for you. (See chapter 31 for more information.)

TAX AVERAGING

The final option is to take the lump sum distribution and average the taxes. Under the IRS tax-averaging provisions, an individual may calculate the tax on a lump-sum distribution as if he/she had received a the payment over a 10-year period. Although he/she still must pay the total tax liability in the first year, spreading the tax liability over a ten-year period can reduce the tax rate and provide substantial savings.

Generally, the larger the lump sum distribution, the less the tax saving. To be eligible, an individual must have been born before January 1, 1936, have participated in the plan for a minimum of five years before the year of distribution and reached age 59 and a half. Many rules and restrictions complicate tax averaging. So, if you think you qualify for 10-year averaging, consult with your tax advisor to see which tax option would be most advantageous.

CHAPTER 30

The NUA Advantage
Company Stock in Retirement Plans

Every advantage has its tax.
– RALPH WALDO EMERSON –
POET

One of the most lucrative tax loopholes arises employees of publicly traded companies retire. It is called the NUA advantage and is contained in Internal Revenue Code Section 402(a).

The opportunity comes from the fact that many employers offer their employees the right to purchase company stock to employees for purchase through their 401(k), profit sharing or other retirement plans. If your plan has been buying your company's stock and the value of the stock has increased substantially in value, you might be eligible for the NUA advantage.

WHAT IS NUA?

NUA stands for *"Net Unrealized Appreciation."* Net unrealized appreciation is the gain in value of your company stock from the time it was purchased for your retirement account until now.

WHAT IS THE NUA ADVANTAGE?

Essentially, the NUA advantage is that you may, under certain circumstances, withdraw stock from your company retirement account and pay either little or no tax, or pay tax at a later date at a drastically lower tax rate.

HOW TO CALCULATE NUA

Let's say you are about to retire after working for the telephone company for the past thirty years. You started buying stock in the pension plan 30 years ago (when you joined the company) when it was worth $1.50 per share (adjusted for all the subsequent stock splits.) Today the stock is worth $41.50 per share.

You have NUA of $40 per share, which is calculated as follows:

Current market value of 1 share of your Company's stock	$41.50
MINUS the original cost to purchase the stock for your retirement account	(1.50)
Net Unrealized Appreciation	$40.00

WHY NUA MATTERS

Normally, when you make a withdrawal from a company retirement plan or IRA, the amount you receive is considered "ordinary income," which is taxable at rates as high as 38.6%. If you qualify for the NUA advantage, the IRS will often allow you to withdraw company stock held in your retirement accounts and pay tax only on the original cost basis instead of the current market value.

As a result, no tax will be due on any gain until the stock is sold. When the stock is sold, it will usually be taxed as a long-term capital gain, which carries a much lower tax rate.

HOW MUCH WILL THE NUA ADVANTAGE LOWER YOUR TAXES ?

Often, the NUA advantage will cut your taxes to roughly half what they would have been had you taken a normal retirement distribution.

An Example of Doing it Right

MILLIONAIRE STORY

Lesson: Take Advantage of Tax Breaks on NUA

NAME:	Jenny
AGE:	62
NET WORTH:	$1.2 million

Jenny was about to retire from a major oil company in Houston and her plan was to retire to the country. She had inherited 71 acres of family land in the part of Texas best known for its beautiful rolling hills and its springtime wildflowers. Along with the family land Jenny also inherited the old "home place" as she called it.

The "home place" was a modest sized house in need of major renovations. She estimated it would cost about $100,000 to get it fixed.

The first thing we did was to inventory her retirement accounts. In her company 401(k) account, Jenny had about $500,000 in company stock. The stock had an original cost basis ranging from a low of $1.50 per share (bought 30 years ago) to $45.00 per share (for more recently purchased stock.)

Jenny, like many retirees, did not want any debts and preferred to pay cash for the home renovations. She had two options:

A. She could rollover her 401(k) to an IRA account when she retired and take a cash withdrawal of $156,000 from the IRA. This would cover $100,000 for home renovations plus another $56,000 to pay the income taxes on the withdrawal, or

B. She could withdraw $125,000 of company stock certificates directly from her 401 (k) account (after she retired but before she rolled over her 401(k) into an IRA.) The lower tax rates for NUA capital gains would net Jenny the $100,000 for the home renovations, but cost her only $25,000 in taxes.

The NUA rules allow you to specifically designate which shares you wish to withdraw from your account. In Jenny's case, she chose to withdraw stock that had a cost basis of only $1.50 per share , even though at the time of withdrawal, company stock was selling for almost $45.00 per share.

By using the NUA advantage, Jenny reduced her taxes from $56,000 to $25,000—a savings of $31,000 or 55 percent.

An Example of Doing It Wrong

MILLIONAIRE STORY

NAME: Joe
AGE: 62
NET WORTH: $2.9 million

Before his retirement, Joe was a PhD engineer in Houston. He was a very intelligent man who prided himself on managing all of his own financial affairs. He also managed to double the amount of taxes he paid in retirement because he did not get professional advice before making a major decision.

I met Joe after a retirement seminar I held for his credit union. Joe had already retired, but asked if I would meet with him to "confirm" (as he said) his retirement decisions. This was destined to be an interesting meeting.

Before retirement, Joe and his stockbroker decided to rollover his entire 401 (k) account to his IRA.

To ensure a productive meeting with Joe, I asked that he bring along his retirement forms, tax returns, and IRA statements. In reviewing those records, I noticed that before the rollover, Joe had $900,000 in company stock in his 401(k) account, which had an original cost basis of roughly $200,000.

Joe also had about $2 million in investments (stocks, bonds and rental properties) outside his IRA, which kept him in a nearly 40% tax bracket.

THE BIG MISTAKE

Joe's decision to cash out his company stock and roll the proceeds into an IRA, left him with no further options. Joe will be required to pay ordinary income tax on all the money that he rolled over (plus all of its future growth) when the money is withdrawn.

At current tax rates, it will cost Joe approximately $360,000 in tax to withdraw his $900,000 in retirement stock value. Had Joe withdrawn these funds as stock certificates while they were still in his 401(k), Joe would have paid only $80,000 in taxes in the year of his retirement...a savings of 78%.

Under current rates, if Joe, had been allowed to sell his stock years later under the NUA advantage, his taxes would have been less than half of what they actually will be as a regular IRA withdrawal. Joe's savings would have been over 50%.

But that's not even the worst part. In Joe's case, his mistake is likely to cost him millions in extra taxes. Why? Because all future growth in his IRA account will also be taxed at rates as high as 40%. Had he used the NUA advantage, the growth would have been taxed only at a 15% rate.

GET PROFESSIONAL HELP

What is the moral of this story? If you have a retirement plan that has been buying your company's stock, find out if you qualify for the NUA tax loophole. Consult a tax advisor who is experienced in this area. The rules are so complicated that people frequently make critical and costly mistakes because they made important decisions without the benefit of professional help.

CHAPTER 31

Roth IRAs

I've been rich and I've been poor.
Rich is better.

– SOPHIE TUCKER –
SINGER

The Roth IRA offers different tax benefits than a regular IRA. Unlike a regular IRA, the Roth IRA does not allow you to take tax deductions on your contributions to your retirement plan. It does, however, allow all earnings to be tax free when you or your beneficiary withdraw them. The chief advantage of the Roth IRA is obvious: the ability to have investment earnings escape taxation at the time you receive them. The advantage comes at a price, however, you don't get a tax deduction when you contribute to the Roth IRA.

A traditional IRA can be converted, partially or entirely, to a Roth IRA if the following conditions are met:

- Your Modified Adjusted Gross Income (MAGI) does not exceed $100,000 in the year of conversion.
- If you are married, taxes are filed jointly.

The converted amount, excluding non-deductible contributions, is included in your income in the year of the Roth IRA conversion.

In determining whether a Roth IRA is the right choice for you, several factors should be weighed. They include your current tax rate, present income, future income, ability to pay taxes due upon conversion of funds outside your IRA, and the size of your estate. Also consider that traditional IRAs prohibit contributions after age 70 and a half, while Roth IRAs allow you to contribute as long as you live, provided you have earned income.

Are Roth IRAs appropriate for retirees? I personally think that they should always be considered because they are a significant way to leverage multi-generational tax planning. In other words, you can leave a Roth IRA to your child or grandchild, income tax free.

To avoid tax on income, many investors buy municipal bonds that typically pay very low rates of interest. However, a Roth IRA can provide the vehicle in which you can buy investments with the potential for far greater returns and still do so free of income tax.

Additionally, if you have a regular IRA, your minimum distribution must be taken at age 70 and a half. You are then must take distributions every year. With a Roth IRA, no minimum income distributions are required regardless of your age. As a result, so you can leave children or grandchildren monies that will always be tax-free.

I had a client who at age 65, didn't think he would live more than eight (8) years. His goal was to leave some money to his son.

My solution was to set aside $50,000 in a Roth IRA by an IRA conversion. If those funds remained in the Roth for 8 years and then he died, they would pass tax free to his wife. Let's suppose that his wife lives another 16 years and keeps the money in the Roth. At her death, it would go to their son. If he kept it in the Roth for another 10 years, the initial $50,000 investment would have compounded tax-free for 34 years and, assuming a ten percent (10%) rate of return, would be worth over $1.0 million tax-free! The following chart illustrates this point:

Figure 31-1	MULTI-GENERATIONAL ROTH IRA HYPOTHETICAL EXAMPLE OF TAX FREE GROWTH	
Value at time of contribution	$50,000	
Value at Father's Death	$107,179	(1)
Value at Mother's Death	$492,486	(2)
Value at Son's Retirement	$1,277,383	(3)
(1) Assumes 10% growth rate over 8-year term		
(2) Assumes 10% growth rate over 16-year term		
(3) Assumes 10% growth rate over 10-year term		

Of course, this is a hypothetical illustration and is not intended to reflect the actual performance of any particular security.

CHAPTER 32

Tax Avoidance
Appreciated Assests—Private Annuity Trust

Unquestionably, there is progress.
The average American now pays twice as much
in taxes as he formerly got in wages.
— H. L. MENCKEN —
WRITER, CRITIC & HUMORIST

I t has been said that success creates its own problems. This is certainly true in the area of capital gains taxation as illustrated by the following millionaire story.

MILLIONAIRE STORY

Lesson: Consider a Tax Avoidance Trust
To Shelter Assets From Tax on Sale

NAME:	Herb
AGE:	67
NET WORTH:	$5.2 million

Herb, the owner of a midsize business, has made substantial profits investing in real estate.

Several years ago Herb bought farmland at a "fire sale" price. As the local economy improved, so did the value of his farm. It soared to approximately a $700,000 profit on his investment. When Herb decided to sell, he was not pleased that he faced a tax liability of $105,000.

We sheltered Herb's profit from taxes by using a tax avoidance trust.

The use of this trust immediately saved Herb over $100,000 in taxes and will save him an additional several hundred thousand dollars in taxes on the growth of this tax sheltered money over his lifetime.

The lesson to be learned is—when selling a highly appreciated asset, consider a tax avoidance trust prior to the sale. It can save you a bundle in taxes.

In this chapter we will explore one planning technique that the wealthy use to delay or reduce the burden of capital gains taxes: "The Private Annuity Trust." In the next chapter we will examine other types of tax avoidance methods for reducing tax on the sale of appreciated assets, Charitable Trusts and planned Charitable Gifting.

> **The tax laws are constantly changing. Before using any of tax planning techniques, be sure to consult a tax professional experienced in this area.**

BASIC CONCEPTS

First, let me orient you to some basic concepts.

A long term capital gain occurs when we sell an asset that has been held for at least twelve months at profit above its tax-adjusted cost (tax basis.) The asset may be a business we owned, an investment in stocks, or perhaps a piece of real estate.

When we make the sale, both the federal government and many state governments want to tax the gain. . This can bring the total cost of your capital gains tax to as much as 25%.

We will illustrate the capital gains tax effect with a simple example:

We buy a business—1970	$200,000
We later sell the business—2003	$500,000
Our tax Basis (adjusted cost)	$200,000
Our capital gain (profit)	$300,000
Our federal tax on gain—15%	$45,000
Our state tax on gain—10%	$30,000
Our total tax	$75,000
Effective tax rate	25%
Tax as a Percentage of Sales Price	**15%**

The impact of capital gains taxes can be devastating to a business owner who started a business, worked for years to build it up, and now wants to sell it and retire. The impact is no less severe to the investor who made a good stock investment and now faces substantial gains taxes.

If the asset being sold is real estate, the situation can be further complicated when depreciation deductions have been taken against the asset. This occurs because when we sell an asset that has been depreciated, we generally must "recapture" or pay tax on the previous depreciation deduction.

Let's revisit our first example, only this time let's assume we are dealing with a rental property that we have depreciated:

We buy a rental property—1970	$200,000
We later sell the property–2003	$500,000
Depreciation claimed	$150,000
Our tax basis ($200-150)	$50,000
Our total gain ($500-50)	$450,000
Our capital gain	$300,000
Our Gain on depreciation recapture	$150,000
Our federal tax on capital gain @ 15%	$45,000
Our federal tax on depreciation recaptured (estimated)	$41,250

(contnued on the next page)

Our state tax on gain—10%	$45,000
Our total tax	$131,250
Effective tax rate	29.17%
Tax as a Percentage of Sales Price	**26.25%**

Notice that when we factor in depreciation, the taxes jump from $75,000 to $131,250.

Both the capital gains tax and the income tax from depreciation recapture must be paid in full within 90 days of the sale of the asset. But, that's not the end of the story. Capital gains are also added to your other income when you prepare your tax return and calculate your AGI (adjusted gross income.)

Your AGI is a key figure for your taxes because it determines the amount of itemized deductions you can claim. A large capital gain often results in a substantial loss of itemized deductions by raising the "floor" for the deductions claimed such as medical and investment expenses. The result is higher taxes because your expenses cannot be deducted. Higher AGI is also taken into account in calculating your personal exemptions. The higher the AGI, the lower the deduction you can take for personal exemptions.

If you receive Social Security, an additional complication arises. The high AGI created by your capital gain is taken into account in calculating the taxable amount of your Social Security benefit. Thus, the effective tax rate on capital gains can be much higher than the 30% illustrated in our examples.

PRIVATE ANNUITY TRUSTS

A private annuity trust does not eliminate taxes, but it can defer the required tax payments over a long- term period (often decades.) Even better, no interest is payable on the deferred taxes, which essentially means that you can invest or earn interest on the unpaid taxes through your trust and keep the profit.

Chapter Thirty-Two

Several parties involved in private annuity trusts. They are the:

- **Grantor**
  The person who owns the asset to be sold.

- **Beneficiary**
  The family of the asset to be sold.

- **Trustee**
  The person or organization that carries out the provisions of the trust. Usually a trust company.

- **Outside Buyer**
  The independent person or company that wishes to buy the Grantor's asset.

HOW THE TRUST WORKS

Instead of the Grantor selling an asset directly to an Outside Buyer (which would be immediately taxable), the Grantor sells the asset to his/her own Private Annuity Trust.

The Trust pays the Grantor full price for the asset with a long term IOU called an annuity contract. The annuity contract is a promise by the trust that it will payments to the Grantor for the rest of the Grantors life. The annuity is a written agreement issued by the Trust. It is not a commercial annuity sold by an insurance company, but a private promise to pay.

The lifetime payments payable under an annuity contract may be made to a single individual or to a married couple. Typically, payments are delayed until the Grantor is ready to retire.

The Trust sells the asset to an Outside Buyer for cash. Because no cash is immediately payable to the Grantor, no tax is generally due at the time of sale. Taxes are not due until distributions are made to the Grantor , which could be decades in the future. In the meanwhile, the trust has use of the entire sales proceeds for new investments. This structure can be tremendously helpful in managing the tax obligations on a large asset sale. It would be appropriate for a small transaction, because of the cost of legal fees to set up this type of trust. Is this type of technique appropriate for you? Consult your tax and legal advisor.

CHAPTER 33

Tax Avoidance
Appreciated Assets—
Charitable Trusts & Gifting Strategies

Make all you can, save all you can, give all you can.
– JOHN WESLEY –
PREACHER & FOUNDER OF METHODISM

Through hard work, saving and long-term investing, many people have accumulated significant assets to fund their retirement. However, selling highly appreciated assets can generate significant capital gains taxes and no one wants to pay extra taxes!! Fortunately, strategies exist for you to defer capital gains taxes, get charitable deductions, and support charitable organizations.

Using these tactics, you can receive up to 46% savings on each dollar you give. The money you save on your tax bill is money you can give again!

Due to newer tax laws:

- You can now deduct charitable donations to up to 75% of your income. The previous limit was 50%.

- In case of death, your estate can claim charitable deductions for up to 100% of income in the year of death and 100% retroactive for the prior year.

- In case of a gift of appreciated property, the 75% limit is increased by 25% of the taxable capital gain.

The laws in this area are complicated and change frequently. Therefore this is an area where you need the services of a good CPA and attorney.

CRUT

One tool to keep you from paying both capital gains taxes and estate taxes is a Charitable Remainder UniTrust (CRUT) A CRUT is a legal tool that has been a well-established part of the Internal Revenue Code for decades. As a bonus, it can reduce your income taxes while increasing your disposable income. Here's what you do:

- First, choose one or more charities that qualify under the Internal Revenue Code as tax-exempt entities.
- Then, sit down with your attorney and have him/her draft a CRUT.
- Finally, donate some assets to the trust.

In a CRUT, you are legally allowed to retain management rights and can withdraw income that the trust generates until you die.

Because you donated the assets to the CRUT, you are entitled to a charitable deduction, which should save you on your income taxes .

As soon as the trust owns the assets, it can sell them without paying capital gains taxes. Therefore, if you donate a stock with a cost basis of $5 per share but market value of $50 per share, the CRUT would pay no capital gain tax when the stock is sold. Without the CRUT, 15% tax would be payable on the profits.

When you die, the value of the donated assets passes to the charities you selected. The entire amount of the donation is deducted from your estate taxes. The amount of tax savings will depend on the size of the donation; if it is large enough, no estate taxes would be owned.

CHARITABLE LEAD TRUST (CLT)

In a CLT, the charity receives the income from the trust and the principal reverts back to the grantor's beneficiaries (usually children) when the trust ends. The value of your gift to your children is discounted because the total value of the property contributed to the CLT is reduced by present value of the income paid to the charity.

For example let's assume you own an apartment complex that you feel will appreciate rapidly in value over the next ten (10) years. Using a Charitable Lead Trust you can give the property to your children today with a discounted tax cost (by letting the children take possession ten years from now and letting a charity keep rents over the next ten (10) years.)

If you have an asset that you think will appreciate at a rate in excess of the IRS's conservative rate assumptions, the excess appreciation may be transferable to your beneficiaries with little or no gift tax cost.

The chart on the following page shows various gifting strategies and their benefits to you and the charity involved:

Figure 33-1

MATCHING YOUR GOALS WITH CHARITABLE GIVING OPTIONS

Charitable Giving Options / Your Goals	Making a Charitable Gift Now	Making a Charitable Gift Future	Keeping Control of Your Gift	Producing Income for Yourself and/or Other Individual Beneficiaries	Leveraging a Smaller Gift
Your Goals	Outright gift of cash or appreciated property, such as real estate, artwork, or investment assets Charitable lead trust provides income to charity for period of years	Gift at your death through your estate planning documents Charity named as beneficiary of retirement assets or life insurance Charitable remainder trust provides assets to charity after an individual beneficiary's life or after a period of years	Gift under your will or a revocable trust Charity named as beneficiary of retirement assets or life insurance Charitable remainder trust Private foundation Donor advised fund	A charitable remainder annuity trust can provide a fixed stream of income A charitable remainder uni-trust or a pooled income fund can provide a stream of income that fluctuates with investment returns	Life insurance Pooled income fund Charitable gift annuity
Benefits	Charity benefits immediately Outright gifts are simple to make Income tax charitable deduction for an outright gift and for some charitable lead trusts Charitable lead trusts can preserve some lifetime benefits for individual beneficiaries	Charitable deduction reduces income tax for gifts during life and for gifts of retirement assets at death Charitable deduction reduces estate tax for gifts at death	During life, gifts under a will or revocable trust can be altered; remainder trust beneficiaries can be changed Retirement and life insurance beneficiary designations can be changed during life A private foundation may choose a variety of available beneficiaries and, over time, can change the charities that benefit from your gifts With a donor advised fund, you may recommend the charities that benefit from your gift and change your recommendations from time to time	Charitable remainder trusts, gift annuities, and pooled income funds produce income for you, your family, or other individual beneficiaries for a period of years or for life	Donors in good health may purchase a large death benefit for a modest insurance premium Pooled income funds allow participation in large investment pools Gift annuities can produce income for the donor when a remainder trust may not be economical

If you would like to reduce your taxes while helping others, charitable giving is an excellent way to do so. Which structure is right for you?

If you are making a substantial gift and want to supplement your retirement income perhaps you will opt for a Charitable Remainder Unitrust.

If you are making a smaller gift of appreciated stock, perhaps you will just donate the certificates claiming a tax deduction for their full market value.

The point is that the proper strategy to use will be different for everyone so be sure to consult your tax, financial and legal advisors before doing anything in this area.

CHAPTER 34

Gifting Strategies—Family

Recommend virtue to your children;
it alone, not money, can make them happy.
I speak from experience.

– LUDWIG VAN BEETHOVEN –
COMPOSER

The area of giving money to family members is full of challenges as the following millionaire story illustrates.

MILLIONAIRE STORY

Lesson: Do Not Give Large Amounts of Money to Young Children

NAME:	Cindy
AGE:	19
NET WORTH:	$1.5 million

Cindy, a 19-year-old, decided to become a hippie after her parents allowed her to vest in her trust fund at age eighteen.

Very few 18 year olds are mature enough to manage a multi-million dollar estate. Giving large money to young children can attract the wrong types of friends and can create a disaster for the young family member.

A better approach might be to create a trust that allowed the young woman to withdraw $1.00 of trust money for each $1.00 of income she earned. Or in the alternative, a trust could be created that would not allow her to touch the principal of her trust fund until she reached the age of 30, 35 or 40. Unfortunately, none of this was done in Cindy's trust. Cindy, a college drop-out is living the good life until the money runs out.

GIFT AMOUNTS

Making gifts to family members can avoid estate taxes upon your death. Here are the rules:

- The first $11,000 of gifts made to each person in a year is tax-free.

- To qualify for tax-free treatment, gifts must be of "present interest" (a direct cash gift, for instance) rather than "future interest" (such as a gift of cash that goes into a trust fund for later distribution).

- Each spouse may make a gift thereby doubling the yearly exclusion to $22,000

- Lifetime gifts up to $1,000,000 (double that if you're married and excluding the annual $11,000 or $22,000) are essentially tax-free.

- Gift and estate taxes are reduced by a special unified tax credit. Of course, if you use the entire credit for lifetime gifts, none will remain to reduce your estate taxes.

You can give away anything you own—the family business, bonds, real estate, an interest in a partnership, and so on. The taxable value of the gift is based on the fair market value of the property on the date of the gift. The recipient does not have to treat the gift as income.

Lifetime gifts to family members are a proven way to pass business assets to others and save estate taxes as well. With proper structuring of the gifts, total gift and estate taxes can be minimized or even eliminated. A lifetime gift works well because it removes any appreciation in the gift assets from the giver's estate. The ability to give the yearly gifts as described above simplifies transferring assets over a multi-year period.

EDUCATIONAL GIFTS

In addition to straightforward gift giving, the government has provided a way for you to finance a loved one's education. It gives you two options: the Coverdell Education Savings Account and a 529 Plan.

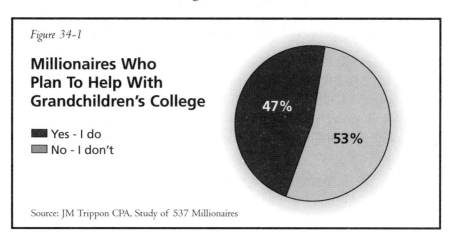

Figure 34-1

Millionaires Who Plan To Help With Grandchildren's College

■ Yes - I do
■ No - I don't

47%

53%

Source: JM Trippon CPA, Study of 537 Millionaires

THE COVERDELL EDUCATION SAVINGS ACCOUNT

The Coverdell Education Savings Account (ESA), formerly known as the Education IRA, allows you to invest up to $2,000 per year for each child until their 18th birthday. Although contributions to ESAs aren't deductible, funds may be withdrawn entirely tax-free if they don't exceed the ESA beneficiary's post-secondary education costs (tuition, fees, room, board, books, and supplies) for that year. ESA funds not used by the time the child turns 30 must be distributed, with the earnings subject to income tax and a 10% penalty. In the alternative, an ESA may be rolled over to an ESA for another family member prior to the beneficiary's 30th birthday,.

529 PLANS

The second alternative is the 529 Plan, which is an investment plan operated by a state that is designed to help families save for future college costs. As with the ESA, the 529 investment grows tax-free and distribution of the funds are also tax-free. This provision is subject to potential sunset revisions on December 31, 2010. At that time Congress may change the tax-free withdrawal status for qualified education expenses. Another feature of the 529 is that the beneficiary has no rights to the funds. You remain in complete control of all funds, decide when withdrawals should be made and for what purpose.

The biggest difference between the educational gift alternatives is the amount that can be saved per beneficiary. Depending upon the state, amounts over $200,000 can currently be held in 529 plans and there are no age or income restrictions. For estate tax purposes, contributions up to $11,000 qualify for the annual gift tax exclusion. Additionally, you can contribute up to $55,000 and elect to treat the contribution as though it was made over a 5-year period.

CHAPTER 35

Tax Payment Planning

The taxpayer;
that's someone who works for the Federal government,
but doesn't have to take a civil service examination.

– RONALD REAGAN –
FORTIETH PRESIDENT OF THE UNITED STATES

The final area of taxation to discuss is tax payment planning. Unless you plan, an IRS surprise could be waiting for the newly retired.

When you retire, *you* will be responsible for making timely and adequate estimated tax payments to the IRS on your retirement income.

When you were working, these payments were usually taken out of your earnings and deposited directly by your employer. At retirement, however, making payments is your obligation.

THE NEED FOR A PLAN

Failure to make your estimated tax payments properly can expose you to substantial penalties. Therefore, it is essential that you become familiar with the rules. If you make a mistake, you may be stuck paying not only the taxes, but penalties also. How big are the penalties? They can be equivalent to an interest rate of 60%, compounded daily. So let's get started.

When you retire you may have several sources from which to pay your living expenses. For example, cash savings, interest income, stock dividends, capital gains, pension annuities, qualified plan withdrawals, social security, and IRA accounts.

If you simply withdraw money from your regular checking account, no tax is generally due because you have already paid tax on the money before it went into your account

The same is not true for other sources of income.

All right, you may say that you already know this. But did you know that the tax rates vary based on the type of income? For example, interest, dividends, pension annuities and most IRA withdrawals are considered ordinary income and are taxed at your marginal tax rate. On the other hand, capital gains, social security and some types of qualified plan withdrawals can be taxed at preferentially lower rates - often 30% to 50% lower than your normal bracket. Because of the complicated nature of tax by income type, it is wise to plan how you will pay for these taxes.

WHEN TAXES ARE DUE

The starting point for a tax payment plan is to know when taxes are due. If you are a US citizen or a permanent resident, estimated tax payments are due on a quarterly basis. The government's quarterly deadlines are different than normal calendar quarters.

The quarterly estimated tax payments are due no later than the following dates:

Quarter	Due Date
1st Quarter	April 15th
2nd Quarter	June 15th
3rd Quarter	September 15th
4th Quarter	January 15th

If you make adequate estimated tax payments on or before these dates you will be fine and incur no penalties.

If you make payments after the above dates, but before the April 15th Form1040 filing deadline, you will owe interest, the amount of which will vary on the basis of the credit markets (currently about 7%).

If you have not paid all estimated amounts (payments and any penalties) by the April 15th Form1040 filing deadline, your penalties jump to a 60% effective annual rate.

HOW TO MAKE THE PAYMENT

You can make your estimated payments in two ways without incurring penalty. You can either:

- Mail you payment with a Form 1040 ES Payment Coupon, or
- Have the income withheld at the payment source (such as by your IRA custodian or company pension department.)

Personally, I think it is easier to use the second method, which is to have your IRA custodian withhold your payments and remit them to the IRS. It's usually best because this system most closely resembles the procedure that you were used to prior to retirement.

HOW MUCH SHOULD YOU PAY

The current law says you are generally responsible for paying the smaller of:

1. 90% of the tax which will eventually be due on this years tax return, or
2. 100% of the tax which was due on your previous years tax return, unless
3. Your income for the prior year was more than $150,000, in which case you must pay 110% of the tax that was due on your previous year's tax return.

I suggest that you have your tax accountant estimate this amount for you because the calculation can get complicated and laws do change. You wouldn't want make a costly mistake.

DISABILITY
AND
ESTATE
PLANNING

CHAPTER 36

Investment During Illness and Disability

A stockbroker urged me to buy a stock
that would triple its value every year. I told him,
"At my age, I don't even buy green bananas."
—CLAUDE D. PEPPER—
WRITER

If you were too ill to manage your investments, who would manage them for you? Your spouse? Your children? Are you sure? We really never know what the future will bring, as the following millionaire story illustrates.

MILLIONAIRE STORY

Lesson: Plan for Investment During Illness and Disability

NAME:	Michael
AGE:	53
NET WORTH:	$4.2 million

Michael, a real estate developer, was diagnosed two years ago with Multiple Sclerosis. This terrible disease will eventually result in Michael's total inability to manage his own affairs. Michael, however, already has executed the appropriate powers of attorney and a trust to manage his assets when he is incapacitated. Michael's foresight and planning will save his family substantial expenses as well as tremendous emotional heartache.

The lesson to be learned is you must create a plan to manage your assets in case you become disabled and your plan must be put in place well before disaster strikes.

Having a seamless transition plan in place to manage your investments if you become ill or incapacitated is commonly overlooked in retirement planning . This chapter will discuss the need for a suitable plan and how to implement it.

NINE REASONS YOU NEED AN INVESTMENT TRANSITION PLAN FOR ILLNESS OR INCAPACITY.

If you are incapacitated and do not have a retirement transition plan for illness and/or disability :

1. You will have abdicated control of how your money will be managed.
2. You may create substantial personal and financial stress for your family.
3. Your accounts could be frozen while court proceedings decide who will manage your affairs.
4. Your family may not know where to locate all of your assets when they need them to cover your healthcare costs.
5. Your Guardian may dispose of your best investments and put the money into something safe like a non-interest bearing checking account.
6. Your income taxes may skyrocket when your portfolio is restructured.
7. Your assets may be depleted by charges levied when a court appointed guardian is assigned to manage your financial affairs.
8. You cannot name a family member or trusted friend to manage your assets in accordance with your wishes.

9. It will be too late for you to explain or advise on how you want
your assets managed .

Most potential clients I meet assume that if they become ill, a family
member would step right in and manage their investment portfolio. To
them, it sounds like a reasonable and practical solution. Unfortunately,
unless you have taken specific steps to document and record your
wishes, it is more likely that your assets will end up in a passbook
savings account controlled by a Court or, worse yet, controlled by a
Guardian chosen by your local Judge, who will bill your account steeply
for "management fees."

Generally speaking, to manage your own financial affairs you must be of
"sound mind." Therefore, if you become so ill that you are unable to
make reasonable decisions, one of three things will occur:

1. If you have executed a power of attorney, the person you pre-des-
   ignated will take over the management of your financial affairs, or

2. If you have executed a living trust agreement, the a co-trustee or
   successor trustee you designate will take over the management of
   your financial affairs, or

3. If you have executed neither of the above, a Judge will take control
   of your assets and will appoint a Guardian to manage your affairs.
   The Guardian may be someone you know (such as your spouse) or
   may be someone you have never met. Often, it will be an attorney
   who knows the Judge but not you. Guardians, seldom have any idea
   of your goals and investment objectives. Many of those who are
   appointed by the courts, perform as Guardians for a living.
   Therefore, they will charge substantially for their services, which
   will reduce the assets in your estate. Guardians will often protect
   themselves from potential suits by your family for losing your
   money by selling your investments and putting them into "something safe" like bank savings accounts.

GUARDIAN PROBLEMS

FORMER MILLIONAIRE STORY

NAME:	Tami
AGE:	22
NET WORTH:	$200,000

(formerly $1.2 million)

The worse case of financial abuse I have ever seen involved an orphaned child. Upon the death of her parent, the court appointed a Guardian to take control of the money left in inheritance (more than a million dollars.) The guardian spent it all on herself. In other words, she stole it. There was supposed to be a fidelity bond posted to protect the orphaned child's money, but the Guardian never arranged for one.

I was called in, after the fact to be an expert witness in the lawsuit seeking to recover the funds. Unfortunately, no funds were ever recovered. You would not want this to happen to your child!

A more common problem with guardianships is that Guardians are often appointed who are completely unprepared to properly perform their duties. Guardians should have experience and understand financial matters and the business atmosphere. The job can be complex because it can involve numerous and widespread claims and assets. The assets alone could take a Guardian months or even years just to locate .

Guardians often create unnecessary tax liabilities by selling investments and putting the proceeds into something "safe" like the bank. Investments you would never have sold because you were depending on them to pay your retirement expenses, can be disposed of without a second thought. The proceeds are often placed in low yielding investments because Guardians' wish to avoid liability for possible investment losses.

Just because you are sick does not mean that your expenses will decrease. Frequently, your expenses will increase substantially due to your medical care. Plus, you must budget to add in Guardian's fees to your expenses. If the Guardian adjusted your portfolio, you may also have to pay significant tax liabilities on the reallocation.

Your income? Remember that may have dropped like a rock, because your Guardian (out of an abundance of caution) has liquidated your portfolio and moved all the money into a passbook savings account at the local bank.

At this point, instead of living off your income, you are forced to begin depleting your principal. Your expenses increase at the same time your income drops. It's not a pretty picture but, unfortunately, it happens all of the time.

What is the solution? The solution is preparation—having a transition plan for your investment portfolio in place in case by become incapacitated.

EIGHT-STEP PLAN

The following is my eight-step plan for maintaining investment continuity in case of illness:

1. Have a properly prepared and executed Durable Power of Attorney. Hire an experienced lawyer to draft and supervise the execution of the Durable Power of Attorney to be sure it is written and signed correctly.

2. If your attorney deems it appropriate, have him/her prepare and supervise the execution of a Living Trust agreement that designates a successor trustees.

3. Name several successors for the persons designated in both your Durable Power of Attorney and your Living Trust. They will serve in the event that the people you designate cannot serve.

4. If it is legal in your state, execute a "Designation of Guardian" form so that if you need a Guardian, you are the one to predesignate who will serve.

5. Verify that your brokerage firms and banks will accept your documents designating your successor. If accepted, place a copy in your files. If they do not accept your documents, obtain their "in house" forms. Complete their forms and place copies in your files and with your designated successor and your attorney.

6. Prepare an inventory of all your investment accounts, account numbers and relevant advisors along with their telephone numbers.

7. Meet personally with the person you designated as your successor. Review the forms, your investment inventory and your investment management/continuity wishes. It is not fair to them or in your own best interests to keep them in the dark. Place an extra copy of all forms and documents in your files and give a duplicate copy to your family attorney, as well as to the person you designated.

8. If you name a bank or trust company as your successor, be sure to verify what the fees that will be charged. Costs can vary greatly from company to company.

CHAPTER 37

Death and Taxes

I got you Babe.
"They say we're young and we don't know
Won't find out until we grow
Well, I don't know, babe, if that's true
'Cause you got me and, baby, I got you Babe,
I got you babe"
– SONNY BONO –
MUSICIAN & CONGRESSMAN

NO SONNY, WE'VE GOT YOU BABE—IRS

Congressman Sonny Bono died without a will

Do you want to hear some really bad news? When you die, you truly can't take your money with you. But, that does not mean that you want to be ravished by taxes when you die.

MILLIONAIRE STORY

Lesson: Estate Planning

NAME:	John Rockefeller, Jr. and Elvis Presley
NET WORTH:	$160 million for John Rockefeller, Jr.
	$10 million for Elvis Presley

Estate planning is what determines how much of your life savings remains to your family and how much goes to the government, as is illustrated by the stories of these two celebrated individuals. John Rockefeller, Jr. died with an estate valued over $160 million, and yet because he did planning and utilized trusts, he had an estate settlement cost of only 16 percent.

Elvis Presley died with an estate of $10 million, and yet lost 73 percent in probate and state settlement costs. The lesson to be learned is that the amount of planning you do determines where your estate goes.

Getting ravished by taxes at death is very common. When married people die, their estates often lose about half their value because of taxes and estate costs. The estates of single or widowed people can lose as much as 70%. Many millionaires fail to stay on top of their estate planning, as the following diagram illustrates.

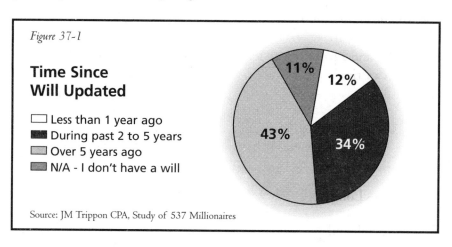

Figure 37-1

Time Since Will Updated

☐ Less than 1 year ago
■ During past 2 to 5 years
☐ Over 5 years ago
▨ N/A - I don't have a will

11%   12%   43%   34%

Source: JM Trippon CPA, Study of 537 Millionaires

Our goal is to use wise planning to legally improve your tax liability at the time of your death. Federal gift and estate tax law permits each taxpayer to transfer a certain amount of assets free from tax during his or her lifetime or at death.

A famous Federal Judge, the Honorable Learned Hand, once said that there are two systems of tax in this country: one for the informed and one for the uninformed.

We have all heard stories about the guy working at Wal-Mart who pays over 30 percent of his wages in taxes and billionaires like the Ross Perot of the world who we are told pay only about 12 percent. Why? Because of loopholes.

However, even the rich can be unaware of the loopholes that can be used to their advantage. Consider Ogden Mills, a former Secretary of the U.S. Treasury. He had a $9.5 million estate at the time of his death and lost 60 percent of it to taxes. Mills worked for the Treasury and in death gave his estate back to the Treasury.

Louis Brandeis, a former U.S. Supreme Court Judge, was asked what the difference was between tax planning and tax evasion. His explanation was as follows:

"Washington, D.C. is across the Potomac River from where I live. I live in Virginia. So, if I have to get downtown in a hurry, I go through the toll bridge and I pay the toll, and I get down there really quick. If I have a little extra time, I'll take the free bridge. It's about 20 minutes out of my way. "

> **"Tax planning is taking the time to find the free bridge. Tax evasion is if you take the toll bridge, but don't stop to pay the toll."**
>
> **— Louis Brandeis, US Supreme Court Judge**

Taxes at death and on estates are areas that are always changing. Planning for taxes and estates requires the help of a good CPA or tax attorney plus an attorney who specializes in estate planning.

REDUCING TAXES

The following are methods used to reduce the burdens of death and estate taxes:

Lifetime Gifts

Gifts given during your life, which are discussed in Chapters 33 (Gifting Strategies—Charities) and 34 (Gifting Strategies—Family) can reduce your taxes at death.

Bypass Trusts

Federal tax law generally permits you to transfer assets to your spouse without incurring gift or estate taxes. Marital deductions, however may increase the federal estate tax liability of the surviving spouse. To avoid this problem, many couples choose to establish a bypass trust.

Bypass trusts can give a husband and wife the advantages of the marital deduction while utilizing the unified credit to its fullest. (The unified credit is an amount which the IRS allows you to leave estate and gift tax free to your beneficiaries either during your life or after death.) With a bypass or credit shelter trust, the first spouse to die can leave the amount shielded by the unified credit to the trust.

For example, if you are a married person and die, both you and your spouse can each designate assets of up to $1.0 million (increasing to $2.0 million in 2006) that would fund a bypass trust which will eventually pass estate tax free to your children.

If only one spouse dies, the trust can provide income to the surviving spouse for life and when the surviving spouse dies, the assets will be distributed to beneficiaries, such as children.

Because both partners made use of their unified credits, the couple is able to pass on a substantial estate tax free to their beneficiaries.

Charitable Gifts

Gifts to charities are not taxed as long as the contribution is made to an organization that operates for religious, charitable or educational purposes. You, or your estate may be entitled to a tax deduction for contribution to a qualifying charity. See Chapter 33.

Chapter Thirty-Seven

Life Insurance Trusts

Life Insurance Trusts can be designed to keep the proceeds of a life insurance policy out of your estate and give your estate the liquidity it needs. To avoid inclusion in your estate, such trusts must be irrevocable—meaning that you cannot dissolve or change the terms of the trust after it is signed. With proper planning, the proceeds from life insurance held by the trust may pass to trust beneficiaries without income or estate taxes.

The above list is subject to changes in law. Remember that the only guaranteed in life is death and taxes. If you are proactive; however, your taxes can be substantially reduced.

CHAPTER 38

Wills and Living Trusts

There's no reason to be the richest man in the cemetery.
You can't do any business from there.

– COL. HARLAND SANDERS –

BUSINESSMAN & FOUNDER OF KENTUCKY FRIED CHICKEN

Every American over the age of 18 should have either a Will, a Living Trust, or both. Which of these documents is right for you will depend on where you reside and your personal circumstances. It might surprise you to learn that even multi-millionaires often ignore this important area of planning.

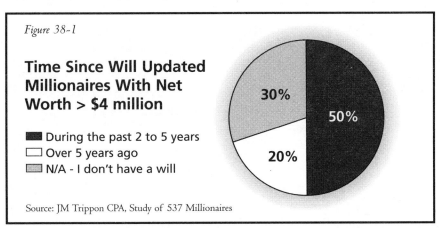

Figure 38-1

Time Since Will Updated Millionaires With Net Worth > $4 million

■ During the past 2 to 5 years
☐ Over 5 years ago
▨ N/A - I don't have a will

30%
50%
20%

Source: JM Trippon CPA, Study of 537 Millionaires

I believe strongly that you must have personal professional advice to write wills and living trusts. If you have followed my guidelines for assembling a financial team, you will have put together a group of advisors, which includes an attorney. This chapter is intended to facilitate your discussion with your attorney, not to replace that discussion.

MILLIONAIRE STORY

Lesson: Don't Do Estate Planning Half Way

NAME:	Serina
AGE:	55
NET WORTH:	$1.9 million

Serina set up an estate plan for her 87 year old mother using a complex series of trusts that if used according to the design would have legally cut her mother's death taxes by over $3 million.

A year after setting up the trust Serina found that the plan was too complicated to follow and she decided to unravel the trust.

Unfortunately, unraveling the trust resulted in more taxes and expenses than had she never set up the trust to begin with. The lesson is that you should not set up a complex estate plan unless you plan to follow through and complete it.

I do not believe in self-prepared wills or "do it yourself" legal software for computer generated wills. Get yourself a real lawyer to draft your will. To prepare for your meeting with your lawyer, review the basic issues surrounding Wills and Living Trusts that follow.

WILLS

A will is a document in which you state how you want your assets to be distributed when you die. It can also express your wishes regarding the raising of children or the management of your funds after your death. Wills typically contain general bequests such as, "I leave everything to my beloved spouse, Kim."

Wills can also contain specific bequests such as "I leave my stamp collection to cousin Suzy." Many wills contain both general and specific bequests.

When preparing your will, your attorney will ask you where and when you want your assets to be distributed. These questions can be of critical importance when young beneficiaries will be involved. In most states, a child is considered to be an adult at age 18. Unless you take steps to the contrary, most beneficiaries will be entitled to receive their inheritance in a lump-sum at age 18. Think about that. Is it prudent to leave a large inheritance to an 18 year old?

I recommend that you place limitations on distributions to children or young adults. For example, your will might restrict distributions to a child or young adult as follows:

- The beneficiary's share of the estate shall be held in trust managed by family member A or, should A decline or be unable to serve, by "XYZ Trust Company."

- Distributions to the beneficiary shall only be in amounts required for the beneficiary's health, education, maintenance, and support. If the beneficiary has not reached age 35, no distribution, in any twelve-month period, may be in an amount that exceeds 5% of the estate's value .

- When the beneficiary ceases to be a full time student (limited to a maximum of 8 years of post high school study), the beneficiary may make no withdrawals from the trust, except for healthcare until age 35. Upon reaching age 35, the beneficiary may withdraw up to 10% of the principal of the estate each 12-month period.

Your attorney knows the appropriate wording to comply with local and state law.

Advantages of Having a Will

1. Generally cheap, easy and fast to create.

2. Avoids dying without a will—also known as dying "intestate." You don't want to die without a will because it could put your family through a nightmare of expense and lots of red tape.

3. Dying without a will places the distribution of your assets with a court. Distribution by a court can be expensive. Your assets may not be distributed to the people you would want to receive them.

Disadvantages of Having a Will Versus a Living Trust

1. A will results in a court process called probate, which can be expensive and open to challenge between beneficiaries.

2. A will does not provide privacy regarding the holdings in your estate. An itemized list of all your belongings is filed into the public records.

3. A will does not address large assets such as retirement accounts and life insurance policies. They are transferred in accordance with the beneficiary designation elections that you made with the retirement custodian or insurance company.

LIVING TRUST

A Living Trust is a legal device that you create to hold your assets both while you are alive and after your death. During your lifetime, you have the right to control your living trust and its assets.

It works like this: you form the trust and transfer assets into it while you are alive. Although you have transferred assets into the trust, you have access to them, and to the income they produce, during your lifetime. Normally, your trust will survive your death and hold the assets for the use of your beneficiaries such as your surviving spouse or children and grandchildren.

When you create a Living Trust, you usually will want to write a "Pour Over Will." The "Pour Over Will" deals with assets that are outside of your Living Trust at the time of your death. The Pour Over moves (or "pours over") assets outside of the Trust, into the Trust, which assures continuity in management and distribution according to the terms of the trust.

Chapter Thirty-Eight

Advantages of a Living Trust

1. Avoids the need to have a Guardian appointed to in manage your assets if you are not healthy enough to handle your own financial affairs. In the Living Trust, you predesignate who will manage the assets if you become physically unable to do so.

2. Avoids probate, which can be time consuming and expensive.

3. Reduces the likelihood that your estate will be successfully contested.

4. Does not disclose your assets. With a Living Trust, inventory of your assets is not required to be filed for public viewing when you die.

Disadvantages of Having a Living Trust Versus a Will

1. Can be expensive and time consuming to create.

2. Requires you to transfer assets into the Trust by either changing the titles on financial and investment accounts or (in the case of real estate) having new Deeds prepared and filing them with the proper authorities.

Many people who spend money to create Living Trusts never transfer their assets into them, which can leave them in a worse position than if they simply had a will. If you create a Living trust, follow all the transfer instructions your attorney prepares for you or you will just be wasting your time and money.

CHAPTER 39

Age- and Behavior-Based Bequests

See, I am setting before you today a blessing and a curse.
– DEUTERONOMY 11:26 –

O ne of the most crucial estate planning decisions is what age or behavior conditions, if any, to place on the access to and use of the assets you bequeath.

A BLESSING OR A CURSE?

Some things can be a blessing or a curse, depending on how you handle them. Inheritances definitely fall into that category.

Risks to avoid:

1. Leaving too much money to someone who is not mature enough to handle it.

2. Denying your heirs the struggles or challenges that will make them strong and self-sufficient.

3. Killing your heirs' ambitions.

4. Condemning your heirs to a life of alcoholism or drug use because they have nothing to look forward to (since they already have it all).

5. Exposing your heirs to being exploited by con-men (or women).

6. Attracting the wrong type of friends.

7. Attracting the wrong type of spouse.

Warren Buffet is quoted as saying the perfect inheritance for an heir is:

"Enough money so that they feel they could do anything,
but not so much that they could do nothing."

MILLIONAIRE STORY

Lesson: Protect Young Children

NAME: John
AGE: 40
NET WORTH: $1.2 million

John, a 40-year-old physician, has two young children, ages 3 and 6.

In his Will, the children will not inherit John's money until age 50. At first glance, this may seem mean-spirited, but it was actually done out of love.

The provisions of John's Will, allow his children to receive the income, interest and dividends from his portfolio until their 50th birthday. However, they cannot consume any of the principal.

John's thinking was simply that an 18-year-old would not be mature enough to manage a substantial estate. Because John wanted his children's' inheritance to be more of a blessing than a curse, he placed age-based restrictions on their ability to access the principal. These restrictions will increase the likelihood that they won't blow their inheritance. The lesson is, do not give young children large inheritances .

THE GOALS

If we spend the time to honestly think about what we want our estate to provide for our family, most of us will probably come up with the following four goals:

I. **To protect our family from ever becoming destitute.**

Usually, there is a difference in the character development of some-one who is "hungry" and someone who is "starving." People tend to grow and become their best when they are challenged (or hungry), but they often lower themselves to desperation or despair when they are "starving." The trick is to find a formula that will challenge your heirs and not leave them destitute.

2. **To provide opportunities for our family.**

   Our hope is that our heirs will turn the assets they inherit into opportunities and combine them with ambition to build productive lives.

3. **To discourage our beneficiaries from developing lazy lifestyles without ambition.**

   Andrew Carnegie remarked, "The parent who leaves his son great wealth generally deadens the talents and energies of the son and tempts him to lead a less useful and less worthy life than he otherwise would."

4. **To minimize arguments and disagreements between the family members we leave behind.**

   We do not want to encourage expensive legal challenges to our estate or to resurrect sibling rivalry or past family feuds.

Age-based Bequests

In most states, a child is legally considered to be an adult at age 18. However, few people of wealth believe that it is prudent to entrust the management of significant wealth to 18 year olds. Furthermore, even when your heirs are older, you should encourage them to live what Carnegie called "useful and worthy lives."

When my wife and I discussed these issues , the first thing we decided was to place age limits on our children's access to our estate after our death. My will states that if I die first, my wife will control all of our assets until her death.

When both of us are gone, our estate will be divided into equal trusts for our children. The children can do the following:

1. If the children are under age 35 when the last parent dies, they can each withdraw up to 5% of the principal value of their trust, per year, for their "Healthcare, Education, Maintenance and Support."

2. If they are between ages 35 and 45, they can withdraw up to 10% of the principal value of their trust, for any reason they consider appropriate.

3. If they are older than age 45, they can withdraw any amount from their trust they wish.

Of course, we hope that by age 45, our kids will responsible enough to capably handle their inheritances. If by that age they are not, they probably never will be.

Behavior-based Bequests

Another way that parents can help their heirs is by creating Behavior Based Bequests in their estate planning documents. Through the use of incentives, parents can instill worthy values their children and grandchildren.

Examples of behavior-based bequests can include:

1. Reimbursement for educational expenses, but only if a certain grade point average is maintained.

2. Prohibiting disbursements to heirs who have failed a drug test or are addicted to alcohol (except perhaps for of treatment and recovery costs).

3. Conditioning the inheritance of each dollar on each dollar that the beneficiary earns from employment, self-employment or investments.

4. Allowing a certain level of withdrawal for a stay at home parent.

If you wish to impose behavior-based conditions, get expert legal advice. Otherwise, you could create unforeseen negative consequence, fail to fund legitimate needs or risk that the provision will be overturned by future court rulings.

Select an attorney who is an expert in behavior-based conditions and can advise you as to these difficult choices.

OTHER GENERAL ESTATE ISSUES

Wills and Estate Plans are complicated, but vital. Although it is impossible to cover every potential issue related to estates and trusts in this book, here are some additional general issues you may wish to include in your estate documents:

1. Your instructions in the event your heirs suffer physical or mental injury in the future.

2. Your instructions as to whether to require funds to continue to be held in trust after your beneficiaries reach age 18, 35, or 45 to protect the assets from future divorce and future ex-spouses.

3. Your instructions regarding whether to require funds to continue to be held in trust and only allowing withdrawals of income. By keeping your heirs from withdrawing principal, you can prevent them from overspending, pledging their inheritance for loans or loss to creditors.

THE NEED FOR A GOOD LAWYER

Hire a competent attorney draft your will and estate documents. If your estate exceeds $1 million, I recommend that any attorney you work with be "Board Certified" in estate planning. Do not try and cut corners by drafting these highly technical documents yourself or by using a do-it-yourself software program. The likelihood of making mistakes, which could cost your estate tremendously and/or invalidate your will, is simply not worth it. Get a lawyer who is an expert, consider it a wise investment.

CHAPTER 40

Tax Avoidance Trust at Death
Stretch IRA/ILITS/GRITS/ GRATS/GRUTS

It's good to have money and the things that money can buy,
but it's good, too, to check up once in a while and make sure you
haven't lost the things that money can't buy.

– GEORGE HORACE LATIMER –
WRITER

The key to keeping your estate intact for your beneficiaries is to reduce your estate tax liability through estate planning. Many strategies are available and what is right for your unique situation depends largely on your total net worth and how you want to distribute your assets.

STRETCH IRA

A Stretch IRA is a wealth-transfer strategy that allows you to extend the period of tax- deferred earnings on the assets of an IRA by passing your IRA assets to a younger beneficiary. Stretch IRAs typically can do this over multiple generations.

In the short run, you can use the Stretch IRA to reduce the required withdrawal you must take from the account and you'll cut your current income tax bill. Meanwhile, because you are extending the IRA payout until a future generation retires, you get additional deferral years to compound the earnings growth.

The new rules authorizing Stretch IRAs, let you determine your minimum yearly distribution on the basis of the joint life expectancies of you and a survivor who's at least 10 years your junior. They assume that both you and your survivor will begin receiving distributions at age 70.

Additionally, the new rules allow you to determine your beneficiary up to the time of your death and permit you to select a beneficiary who may be more than 10 years younger than you. As a result, Stretch IRAs reduce the current minimum distribution requirements and extend the deferral period.

A Stretch IRA assumes:

- You don't need the money either before or after retirement.
- You will withdraw the least amount of money legally allowable and at the latest time allowable before you would incur penalties.
- Your primary beneficiaries die before they can deplete the investment fund.
- That tax laws will remain constant.
- That inflation is minimal and that it will not significantly cut into your rate of return and the final value of your account.
- That your returns do not vary.

ILIT (IRREVOCABLE LIFE INSURANCE TRUST)

To keep death benefits out of your estate, set up an ILIT and have it purchase the policy for you. Otherwise, you may be buying twice as much life insurance as you need because, after exemptions (which change from year to year) the Federal Estate Tax is generally going to take 50% of the policy death benefit in taxes.

An ILIT works like this: take your insurance and place it in a trust that you cannot change. Make sure that your spouse is not a direct beneficiary of the insurance. The beauty is that your spouse can be the income beneficiary of the trust and can get principal if he/she needs it. Your spouse, can also be the trustee, which means that he/she can use the trust checkbook and is responsible for interpreting the trust.

GRIT (GRANTOR RETAINED INTEREST TRUST)

A GRIT allows the grantor to transfer the shares of a business to another person for a specified period of time. During the transfer period, the grantor continues to receive income from the trust. At the end of the specified period, the trust terminates and the beneficiary receives ownership of the shares of stock in the business. No tax is paid at that time.

A GRIT may be a viable means of transferring ownership to a successor child in situations in which parents want to retire prior to the time when a child is ready to take control of the business. The business would be transferred, in trust, to an interim person who would manage the business and then ultimately to the child as the beneficiary of the trust.

GRAT (GRANTOR RETAINED ANNUITY TRUST)

A GRAT is basically the same as a GRIT except that the grantor must receive a specified fixed percentage of the value of the assets in the trust for a certain period of time. GRATs are irrevocable trusts that let you transfer income-producing or highly appreciating assets to the trust, yet enjoy an annuity from the assets for the fixed term of the trust.

At least once a year, you, as the grantor, must receive a fixed dollar amount of the assets in trust. After the trust ends, any assets remaining in the trust, after payment of your annuity, go to the beneficiary. Gift tax is payable on the basis of the asset's original value reduced by the present value of your retained annuity and can be substantially less than corresponding estate taxes, if the asset appreciates significantly.

GRUT (GRANTOR RETAINED UNIT TRUST)

A GRUT is similar to a GRAT except that the income received as a percentage of the trust assets must vary annually. A GRUT may be a good vehicle for a grantor who desires flexibility in the amount of income he/she will receive from the trust.

PRIVATE ANNUITY TRUST

A Private Annuity Trust is a method of transferring ownership in a business to your children when you want to receive a steady income stream. Private annuities for family-owned business situations are contracts between the successors, usually children who will inherit the business, and the business owner, the children's parents. They stipulate that in return for transferring ownership of the business to the successors, the business owner will receive income from the business as long as the owner and his/her spouse live. A rather unique form of business sale is created because the actual amount paid by the successors for the business is ultimately determined by how long the owner (and spouse) lives and not by a fixed value. The private annuity concept is not really complicated but as with all such strategies care and planning are vital.

CREDIT SHELTER TRUST

The primary purpose of a credit shelter trust is to fully utilize the unified tax credit allowed to each individual by the Internal Revenue Service. The unified tax credit gives each person a $1 million (scheduled to increase to $2 million by 2006) estate tax credit. In other words, the first $1 million of an individual's estate is not subject to federal estate tax.

With some simple planning and the use of a credit shelter trust, a married couple can pass on $2 million in assets without paying any estate taxes (scheduled to increase to $4 million by 2006). To do so, each spouse establishes a trust with specific assets that equal the amount of the unified tax credit.

Remember that creating a trust may have significant income, gift, or federal estate tax consequences that are too complicated to explain fully here. In addition, tax laws are constantly changing and the changes can affect trust accounts. Have all trusts reviewed by your financial team to determine the tax consequences

CHAPTER 41

Family LTD Partnerships and Estate Planning

God gave me my money. I believe the power to make money is a gift from God to be developed and used to the best of our ability for the good of mankind. Having been endowed with the gift I possess, I believe it is my duty to make money and still more money and to use the money I make for the good of my fellow man according to the dictates of my conscience.

— JOHN D. ROCKEFELLER —
INDUSTRIALIST & PHILANTHROPIST
FOUNFER OF STANDARD OIL

Another estate planning option is a Family Limited Partnership. A Family Limited Partnership (FLP) is a business organization owned by family members, usually with the parents as general partners with full control and risk, and the children as limited partners with no control and limited risk.

Legally, the only distinction between a "Family Limited Partnership" and most other limited partnerships is that in a FLP only family members may participate.

MILLIONAIRE STORY

Lesson: Use of LTD Partnerships in Estate Plans

NAME:	George
AGE:	75
NET WORTH:	$83 million

George, a retired real estate investor, built a substantial net worth, which was primarily held in the form of real estate rental properties.

Upon his death the estate settlement and tax cost would be substantial and could surpass 60 percent of George's net worth.

One potential tool for managing estate taxes is a limited partnership, which often allow taxpayers to reduce the value of estate assets for tax purposes. In George's case, a limited partnership could reduce his estate costs by as much as $4 million. Why? Because the IRS will allow you to gift shares (called units) to your children which reduces your taxable estate and the IRS will allow a reduction in your total estate value for something called a "control discount."

Consult your attorney as to whether or not this is an appropriate move for your situation. The lesson to be learned though is, structuring of your assets will impact their taxes and use of a tool, such as limited partnerships, may have a significant benefit in reducing your estate taxes.

In an FLP, the limited partners are intended to receive complete control of the assets when the general partner dies. When the FLP is formed, the business assets are transferred to the partnership. Those assets can be a family-owned business, real estate, stocks, etc.. By transferring income-producing capital assets (i.e. rental property) into an FLP, the value of the assets can be discounted up to thirty percent or more based on factors such as the lack of marketability of or minority interest in the partnership shares.

The general partner maintains complete control of the partnership business including the distribution of earned income. The limited partners receive their interests by means of gifts from the general partner. A limited partner cannot take assets from the partnership or otherwise force the liquidation of the partnership before its term is up.

Since the limited partners have no control over the business assets, they can receive their shares of the assets at discounted values. The discounted values enable grantors to transfer more asset value to their heirs than could have if the assets were merely inherited and the amounts received were reduced by estate taxes .

The tax advantages of an FLP are even greater when the value of the assets appreciate after the children receive their FLP shares. This occurs because the appreciation is not included in the parents' taxable estate at death. Additionally, the FLP can result in income tax advantages during the parents' lives because the income attributable to FLP shares of children over age 14 is taxed in the children's rather than the parents' bracket.

ADVANTAGES OF FLPS

There are numerous advantages to Family Limited Partnerships. The principal business reasons include:

- Centralized control over the management and investment of family assets.
- Cost savings from consolidating family assets into a single entity.
- Consolidation of investments of real estate into a partnership that allows the property to be developed or managed in an orderly manner
- Avoidance of problems typically created when undivided interests in real estate become owned by multiple parties.
- Asset protection from potential domestic relations problems.
- An effective way to implement a gift-giving program.
- Protection for limited partners against claims of future creditors.
- Avoidance of out-of-state probate since partnership interests are personal property.
- Control over family assets through a buy-sell arrangement included in the partnership agreement.

DISADVANTAGES OF FLPS

- The biggest drawback when establishing a Family Limited Partnership is the cost of establishing and maintaining it. FLPs can be expensive.

- Costs include attorney's fees to set up the partnership and appraisal fees to establish both the underlying value of the partnership shares (also called units) and appropriate discounts.

- In addition, annual accounting fees must be paid for the preparation of the partnership returns. The state may also charge an annual fee for the right to do business as a limited partnership in the state.

Proceed cautiously when setting up an FLP. Several key requirements MUST be attended to correctly to avoid problems with the IRS. Seek professional advice!

CHAPTER 42

Leaving a Legacy

Like good stewards of the manifold grace of God,
serve one another with whatever gift each of you has received.
— I PETER 4:10 —

When considering the final pillar in your financial mansion, we need to seriously reflect on the kind of a person you are and what you stand for in life. Why? Because your loved ones will remember and think about who you were, when you are gone.

When you make your Will, you are providing others with a future. Long after the bequests are spent and the valuables have been stored away in a dark closet, your legacy can live on. The legacy you leave is a rare and special gift from you to others, from one generation to the next.

When I speak of leaving a legacy, I am really addressing your ultimate memory with two groups: your descendants (family) and your community. We have already spent a great deal of time examining the estate planning issues impacting your family. This book would be incomplete however, without also examining your legacy with the second group...your legacy in society.

Each year, billions of dollars and countless hours of volunteer service are donated to support civic and cultural activities, humanitarian programs, education, wildlife protection and preservation, environmental conservation, medical research, religious programs and more. The social benefit of philanthropy touches every class, race, age, religion and economic stratum and will positively influence all future generations.

Charitable, nonprofit groups play an important role in our lives. They extend help in many ways that range from giving seniors a hot meal to linking up children with good role models. Help may also come in the form of battling a terrible disease, leading a spiritual event or bringing beauty to your world through the arts.

Knowing what you stand for—your values, your desires—will strongly influence your charitable contributions. By making these "planned gifts," you can continue to help organizations that are making a major difference in our communities. When you leave a legacy, you insure that help will continue to be available to those who need it.

The involvement of your children in giving decisions is of enormous importance because it teaches them to be socially conscious of giving, serving, and realizing the impact they can have on society. Through your children, your giving may be carried on for generations and the thread of your values may continue to be woven into the fabric of society.

This is why many people establish family foundations, or donor advised funds, so that your children can participate in both the gifting and in maintaining your legacy.

A legacy is a gift for the future—
and for the generations to come.

CHAPTER 43

Putting It into Practice

All our dreams can come true,
if we have the courage to pursue them.

– WALT DISNEY –

CARTOONIST & FILM PRODUCER

W̱ell, we've covered a lot of ground together. Throughout these pages, I have imparted the best practices I have learned from those who have been there—the self-made millionaires I work with every day. We have come though this journey together to a place where you must now make a serious decision. What will you do with your new knowledge?

It is my hope that by training you with millionaire skills, and then introducing you to some new millionaire friends you will have become empowered to make some changes in your life.

You probably have also realized what I learned years ago: millionaires are just ordinary people! They are people who worry about their kids and their health. They are people who go to church, read the paper and walk next to you in the park. But they are also people who manage their money differently than most non-millionaires.

It is my goal that by sharing what I've learned, you will take action and add some good new habits to your financial regimen. I am going to help you do just that!

Because you have done a great job in making it to this point, I have a graduation present for you. If you will come to my Website:

www.stayrichforever.com

and click on the graduate tab, I will make a gift to you of one my special reports that I normally sell for $79.

I will also give you a free subscription to my Stay Rich Forever electronic newsletter, which will bring you a monthly discussion of tips to protect your wealth, reduce your taxes, and preserve your assets. It's my way of encouraging you to apply the information and ideas in this book and to thank you for sharing your time with me.

I hope you join me and Stay Rich Forever.

Jim Trippon CPA
Houston, Texas
October 2003

P. S. If you have any comments, success stories, or ideas for future editions, I would love to hear from you. You can reach me at:

jtrippon@stayrichforever.com

ABOUT *the* AUTHOR

James M. Trippon, CPA, author and financial columnist, has been advising millionaires on wealth accumulation and protection for over twenty years. Trippon manages a branch of Raymond James Financial Services, Incorporated, a member firm of the National Association of Securities Dealers (NASD) and the Securities Investor Protection Corporation (SIPC). His boutique financial advisory firm serves a client base of affluent corporate and individual clients. He has personally interviewed over a thousand millionaires and has advised many of them on aspects of making and maintaining their fortunes. He covers issues such as the critical details of retirement, estate, education funding, portfolio management, advanced tax planning, and pension fund investment management. Prior to opening his own firm, Trippon worked with Price Waterhouse as a senior financial statement auditor for Fortune 100 corporations. Trippon and his family reside in Houston, Texas.

ORDER FORM
Order online at www.stayrichforever.com

How Millionaires Stay Rich Forever audio
  retirement planning workshop
  Six audio CDs...$ 189.95

How Millionaires Stay Rich Forever:
Retirement Planning Secrets of Millionaires
  Hardcover book..$ 21.95

How Millionaires Stay Rich Forever Philosophy
  Single audio CD..$ 16.95

How Millionaires Stay Rich Forever electronic newsletter,
  one-year subscription...FREE

Order all items and save! Includes 7 audio CDs,
  hardcover book and free newsletter — a $228 value!
  Package price...$ 199.95

TOTAL (Please add $3 per item for shipping).......................$_____

GUARANTEE: EVERYTHING we sell comes with a no B.S.,
money-back, *lifetime* guarantee. If you're not happy, send it back!

Name: _____

Company: _____

Address: _____

City:_____State:_____Zip: _____

Phone:_____E-mail:_____

❑ Visa   ❑ MC   ❑ Am Ex   ❑ Personal check
(Make checks payable to Bretton Woods Press)

Acct No._____Exp. Date _____

Signature _____
(Credit card charges will appear as Bretton Woods Press)

Order online at **www.stayrichforever.com** or send this form
along with your check or credit card information by fax to:

Bretton Woods Press LLC • Fax: 713-669-0503 • Phone 800-952-1099
Email inquiries: support@stayrichforever.com

ORDER FORM

Order online at www.stayrichforever.com

How Millionaires Stay Rich Forever audio
   retirement planning workshop
   Six audio CDs...$ 189.95

How Millionaires Stay Rich Forever:
Retirement Planning Secrets of Millionaires
   Hardcover book...$ 21.95

How Millionaires Stay Rich Forever Philosophy
   Single audio CD..$ 16.95

How Millionaires Stay Rich Forever electronic newsletter,
   one-year subscription..FREE

Order all items and save! Includes 7 audio CDs,
   hardcover book and free newsletter — a $228 value!
   Package price ....$ 199.95

TOTAL (Please add $3 per item for shipping)......................$_____

GUARANTEE: EVERYTHING we sell comes with a no B.S.,
money-back, *lifetime* guarantee. If you're not happy, send it back!

Name: _____

Company: _____

Address: _____

City:_____State:_____Zip: _____

Phone:_____E-mail:_____

☐ Visa   ☐ MC   ☐ Am Ex   ☐ Personal check
(Make checks payable to Bretton Woods Press)

Acct No._____Exp. Date _____

Signature _____

(Credit card charges will appear as Bretton Woods Press)

Order online at **www.stayrichforever.com** or send this form
along with your check or credit card information by fax to:

Bretton Woods Press LLC • Fax: 713-669-0503 • Phone 800-952-1099
Email inquiries: support@stayrichforever.com